International Perspectives on Fiscal Fe

The Basque Tax System

Basque Politics Series No. 15

International Perspectives on Fiscal Federalism:
The Basque Tax System

Edited by Gemma Martínez and Xabier Irujo

Center for Basque Studies
University of Nevada, Reno
2018

Basque Politics Series No. 15
Series editor: Xabier Irujo

William A. Douglass Center for Basque Studies
University of Nevada, Reno
Reno, Nevada 89557

Editors:
Gemma Martínez and Xabier Irujo

http://basque.unr.edu

ISBN-13: 978-1-949805-01-7
ISBN-10: 1-949805-01-8

Library of Congress Cataloging-in-Publication Data forthcoming

Contents

Preface

Gemma Martínez and Xabier Irujo

In 2014 the William A. Douglass Center for Basque Studies (CBS) at the University of Nevada, Reno celebrated its thirteenth annual conference, "Fiscal Systems and the Crisis," which proposed the analysis of public finances and self-government in Euskadi, Catalonia, and Nevada in the context of the 2008 financial crisis. In 2017, a compilation of the contributions, providing an analysis of fiscal policies and the evolution of public finances submitted to the conference by distinguished scholars and public officials related to the Basque Country, was published in the book *Basque Fiscal System Contrasted to Nevada and Catalonia: In the Time of Major Crises* by the CBS.

Since then, the CBS has introduced a new knowledge field into its activities: economic and legal studies, with an emphasis on the financial-economic framework of self-government, particularly with regard to the Basque public financing and tax system. In parallel and more specifically in 2016, the Provincial Government of Bizkaia included the promotion and dissemination of international research about the Basque Economic Agreement and comparable federal fiscal systems as a target in its strategic plan of government *Bizkaia Goazen 2030*.

In particular, the Provincial Government of Bizkaia seeks to raise awareness about the Basque tax system by means of international outreach and also to move forward in the understanding of the structural relations between the system of the Basque Economic Agreement and other federal models existing in the United States of America and worldwide. The Center for Basque Studies certainly offers an ideal opportunity to achieve those objectives, given its long track record of excellence in research and publications about the Basques and its commitment to interdisciplinary collaboration.

With the aim of achieving their common goals, the signing of a Collaboration Agreement between UNR and the Government of Bizkaia in 2014 was a remarkable milestone. Pursuant to said agreement, two experts in taxation from the Provincial Government of Bizkaia were seconded for one term in 2015 and in 2016 for the purpose of carrying out research work into comparable federal systems and to showcase the Basque Economic Agreement.

The positive outcome of the two-year Collaboration Agreement led to the signing in 2016 of a new Collaboration Agreement, which will expire in 2019, pursuant to which another two governmental experts were carrying out research work for a term in 2017 and 2018.

In compliance with the agreement, the CBS, with the financial support of the Provincial Government of Bizkaia, organized on April 3 and 4, 2019, a Symposium on Basque Fiscal Systems, within which said Basque public officials offered the results of their research conducted at the CBS. As to enrich the symposium, distinguished scholars from several universities were also invited to offer their views on the topic from different perspectives. The symposium became, thus, a meeting point for the tax practitioners in the Basque institutions and the international academia.

This book—*International Perspectives on Fiscal Federalism: The Basque Tax System*—is a compilation of the eight contributions presented in the symposium. The central thread running through most of the chapters is the analysis of the Basque Economic Agreement as a financial self-government tool for the Basque Country from the perspective of some of the reference federal models in the world: the United States of America, Switzerland, Australia, and Canada.

The two first chapters are devoted to a detailed overview of the most outstanding legal and economic features in both the Basque and the US public revenue systems, and their comparative analysis. In chapter 1, Gemma Martínez Bárbara, Head of the Tax Policy Unit of the Treasury Department in the Provincial Government of Bizkaia, identifies those aspects that can be regarded as common between the federal tax structure in the United States of America and the Basque tax and financial system. She identifies some of the common fundamentals and legal principles of both tax systems, and presents some similarities in both initial tax structures, and also some common trends in the evolution of both models. In chapter 2, Nieves Pereda Chávarri, Deputy

Director of Tax Collection of the Treasury Department of the Provincial Government of Bizkaia, analyses the most relevant economic aspects in the financing of public systems in both intergovernmental models in order to assess their capacity to reach adequate levels of autonomy of sub-central governments, efficiency, income distribution, equity, accountability and others.

Chapters 3 and 4 are focused on two particular aspects of these federal models. Mikel Amuriza Fernandez, a tax inspector in the International Tax Unit of the Treasury Department of the Provincial Government of Bizkaia, tackles tax harmonization and collaboration, one of the hottest topics in international taxation nowadays. He offers an analysis of the federal fiscal system of the United States, in comparison with the European Union, and of the state of Nevada compared with the Basque Country. He also comments on the jurisprudence of the US Supreme Court and of the European Court of Justice on this topic. In Chapter 4, Aitziber Etxebarria Usategi, a public official specializing in Personal Income Tax in the Treasury Department of the Provincial Government of Bizkaia, presents the results of her comparative research on Wealth Transfer Taxes in the Basque Autonomous Community and the United States of America. After an introductory part on the legal regulation of wealth transfers on both systems, the chapter goes through the most important differences between taxes from both territories and explains the harmonization concerns to be taken into account.

Contributions from academia can be found in chapters 5 through 8. Following the comparative thread of the former chapters, Mikel Erkoreka Gonzalez, who holds a doctorate in History from the University of the Basque Country (UPV/EHU) and is manager of the Ituna Center for Basque Economic Agreements and Fiscal Federalism Studies, focuses on comparing the exercise of tax power by Basque and Swiss sub-central governments from a historical perspective. By contrasting the two case studies, the chapter aims to identify key factors involved in nation-state building processes in federal systems. Chapter 6 is authored by Caroline Gray, who holds a PhD in Politics and is a lecturer at Aston University in Birmingham, UK, specializing in sub-state nationalist movements, decentralization, and the political consequences of the global financial crisis of 2008, with a particular focus on the Basque Country. Departing from the most common approach of the Economic Agreement as the instrument that governs financial and fiscal relations between the Basque Country and Spain, her contribution spotlights on the Basque Economic

Agreement as a prototype for the form of bilateral relationship that the Basque Nationalist Party (PNV) seeks to establish in wider political matters, and the challenges it faces at state, supranational, and sub-state levels to achieving this.

In Chapter 7, Sofía Arana Landín, who holds a PhD in International Tax Law from the University of the Basque Country (UPV/EHU) and is Director of International Projects at the same university, proves the great impact of the Economic Agreement on Basque economic development and how it has contributed to the creation of a unique system in which the preservation of traditions becomes intermingled with investing in Innovation, Research, and Development, creating synergies that have proved to be extremely effective and successful and can be considered to be a model of reference. Finally, in Chapter 8, Roberto Bernales Soriano, who holds a PhD in Tax Law from the University of the Basque Country (UPV/EHU) and is Professor of Tax Law at the University of Deusto, bears in mind the case studies of Australia and Canada and identifies the future challenges of the Economic Agreement in relation to a likely devolution of powers to the local government in the twenty-first century in order to tackle current social and economic realities.

In short, this book aims to be a new contribution to knowledge and studies on fiscal federalism and to achieve a better understanding internationally of and a greater visibility for the Basque Economic Agreement.

In February 2018 we celebrated the 140th anniversary of the Basque Economic Agreement. Basque Institutions, political parties, the media, academia, and other stakeholders in Basque society paid extraordinary attention for some days to one of the most and unique instruments of self-government in the Basque Country. Major efforts were made during those days with the intention of spreading its essence and features in Basque society in order to combat the statistical data that show that the Economic Agreement is still unknown for many Basques. Surprisingly, after 140 years impacting on the lives of many generations of Basques, the *Sociómetro* survey released by the Sociological Research Department of the Basque Government reveals that 45 percent of Basque citizens have stated that they have never heard of the Economic Agreement.

History shows the Economic Agreement, with all its weaknesses and its strengths, is not the perfect federal model, but it is the Basque model of governing financial and fiscal relations with the central state based on negotiation and agreement. It is certainly one of the most outstanding signs of Basque identity. Therefore, it is vital to generate strategies that help to raise awareness among Basque society about the relevance of such an instrument as the only way to love and protect it.

Since February 28, 1878, the Economic Agreement has overcome major challenges such as wars, political and economic crises, and dictatorial governments. The twenty-first century brings its particular challenges not only at the state level—strong centralism emerging, blunt attacks against the Economic Agreement, and constitutional crisis—but at the international level as well in the form of globalization, uniformization, and the digital economy and markets.

Initiatives that will help to face such challenges are being promoted and supported by the Provincial Government of Bizkaia, most of them at the domestic level. The Collaboration Agreement in 2014 with the CBS was a step forward into the international arena. After six years and two Collaboration Agreements, the fruitful outcome of this initiative predicts a long term relationship.

Chapter 1

US and Basque Tax Systems: A Comparative Approach to Their Evolution and Legal Fundamentals

Gemma Martínez Bárbara

Drawing parallels between the construction and fundamentals of the federal tax structure in the United States of America and the Basque tax and financial system, the so-called Economic Agreement, is quite an exciting challenge. This chapter aims to take up this challenge and identify those aspects that can be regarded as common to both systems, bearing in mind the existence of great differences between the historical context in which the origin and evolution of each tax model took place.

This analysis presents the similarities that can be found in both initial tax structures as well as some common trends that can be observed in the evolution of both models. In addition, it identifies some of the common fundamentals of both tax systems, which are closely related to the federal features of the US and the Basque legal order, although in the Basque case this federal nature is rejected by those who consider the system one of high but mere fiscal decentralization.

The construction of each model is the result of two very different processes in response to the particular political, legal, and historical contexts of each case. It is also important to bear in mind that the American and Basque tax systems' construction processes were developed in the framework of two completely separate law environments: the common law system and the civil law system.

On the one hand, the common law tradition, generally uncodified and largely based on *precedent* (meaning the judicial decisions that have already been made in similar cases), emerged in England during the Middle Ages and was applied within British colonies, like those in America, across continents. On the other, the civil law tradition, codified and in which the judge's role is to establish the facts of the case and to apply the provisions of the applicable code, developed in continental Europe at the same time as the common law tradition and was applied within the colonies of European imperial powers such as Spain and Portugal.

SIMILARITIES IN BOTH INITIAL TAX STRUCTURES

In the early modern period[1] three common elements—that is, heterogeneity, protectionism, and weak fiscal pressure—can be attributed not only to the tax structures of the British colonies in America but to those of the three Basque provinces—Araba, Bizkaia, and Gipuzkoa—as well.

In both cases, heterogeneity was an outstanding feature. If the British colonies and the Basque provinces had something in common, it was the diversity or the lack of uniformity of taxation. Different modes of political organization were adopted by each state or province and all of them were legally valid.

According to scholars,[2] the economic relations between the colonies, the constituent states of the American Union at the end of the Revolution, closely resembled the situation in the German Confederation after the Congress of Vienna in 1815.

In the case of the British colonies, British tax traditions were diverse, and the various colonies and local communities had a rich array of tax figures from which to choose. Among them were taxes on imports and exports; property taxes (taxes on the value of real and personal assets); poll taxes (taxes levied on citizens without any regard for their property income or any economic characteristics); and excise (sales) taxes and faculty taxes, which were the taxes on the implicit income of people in trade or businesses. The mix varied, but each colony made use of virtually all these different modes of taxation.

---

1   In American historiography the early modern period follows the late Middle Ages of the post-classical era and differentiates between the early modern period, which ended when the French Revolution of the 1790s began, and the modern period to date.
2   Percy Ashley, *Modern Tariff History: Germany, United States, France* (London: J. Murray, 1920) and Frank Taussig, *The Tariff History of the United States* (New York: Putnam's Sons, 1905).

In the case of the Basque provinces,[3] the tax assessment by the farmers or *labradores,* the *prebostades* of the villas, the tax on ironworks, the tax on monasteries and the penalties on chamber, and the sales tax or *alcavala* were, among others, the main duties paid to the lord. However, each of the three provinces chose which duties to levy. For instance, in Bizkaia the sales tax or *alcavala* was not imposed, but in Gipuzkoa this was the main tax duty.

Protectionist policies conditioned both initial tax structures as well. It is worth mentioning that the separate colonies had been allowed by Great Britain to impose customs duties for revenue purposes and had also been influenced somewhat by protectionist ideas. Even after 1776, customs duties continued to be levied by each state against all others.

At that time, there were practically no manufactures to protect because colonies were almost entirely engaged in agriculture and in the occupations, mainly handcrafts, closely connected with it. All manufactured goods that could be imported were not made at home but obtained in exchange for agricultural exports. In addition, the production of unmanufactured iron was carried on to a considerable extent.

The fundamentals of early protectionism in America are collected in Alexander Hamilton's *Report on Manufacturers* (1791) in reply to Congress's requirement of a report on plans for the encouragement of manufacturers to render the United States independent of other nations for essential (particularly military) supplies. There is the argument from the desirability of national self-sufficiency that comprises the means of subsistence, habitation, clothing, and defense. According to Hamilton, the control of these areas is necessary to the perfection of the politic body as well as to the safety and to the welfare of the society.[4] As definite proposals, he recommended the grant of bounties, the free admission of raw materials, the payments of drawbacks, and general protection against all manufactures´ items that could be produced in the country.

---

3   For the historical aspects of the evolution of the Basque tax systems, see, among others, Joseba Agirreazkuenaga, *The Making of the Basque Question* (Reno: Center for Basque Studies, University of Nevada, Reno, 2011); Joseba Agirreazkuenaga and Eduardo Alonso Olea, *The Basque Fiscal System: History, Current Status, and Future Perspectives* (Reno: Center for Basque Studies, University of Nevada, Reno, 2014).

4   Frank W. Taussig, *State Papers and Speeches on the Tariff* (Cambridge, MA: Harvard University, 1892), at http://oll.libertyfund.org/.

Another motto of the protectionists was the young or infant industries argument. According to Frank W. Taussig's reasoning,[5] the argument was, in brief, that it may be advantageous to encourage by means of legislation a branch of industry that may be profitably carried out and, therefore, would eventually be so for sure, but whose growth was prevented for the time being by circumstantial or accidental causes.[6]

Some of the Basque traditional *foral* tax rights were also grounded on protectionism. In particular, the establishment of customs duties for imported products inland and not on the coast had an important economic impact on the trade of products in the Basque provinces. Since the fourteenth century, customs were established for Bizkaia in Orduña and Balmaseda, for Araba in Vitoria-Gasteiz, and for Gipuzkoa in Navarre. As a result, hardly any duty was paid on imported products from abroad and Basque exported products. Duties were not paid until goods entered into Castile or into Navarre. This is one of the reasons why the Basque provinces were known as exempted provinces.

The third common feature relates to fiscal pressure and its evolution. Before the Revolution, Americans were very lightly taxed in peace time. In Britain, taxes were several times higher. Indeed, in the literature promoting British emigration to America the absence of heavy taxation to defray public debts and standing armies was pointed to as something peculiar to America.

In the case of the Basque provinces, they were initially distinguished for their low fiscal pressure compared to the rest of the provinces linked to the kingdom of Castile. To start with, one should note the dual nature of their taxation activity. As foral territories, they had their own political and administrative organization and, in order to fund their expenses, each of them had a certain degree of tax autonomy. In addition to this internal scope, Basque territories, under the political and administrative regime of the King of Castile—the Lordship—since 1379, had to pay the taxes established by the Old Law (Fuero Viejo) of 1452 and updated by the New Law (Fuero Nuevo) in 1526.[7]

---

5   Taussig, *The Tariff History of the United States.*
6   The same mere economic argument was used to ground the rationale of protectionism by the English economist S. Mills and by the German economist F. List.
7   Gregorio Monreal Zia, *The Old Law of Bizkaia* (Reno: Center for Basque Studies, University of Nevada, Reno, 2005).

In fact, their contribution to the king was much lower than those of the other provinces linked to the Crown and was strictly set by the aforementioned laws. This is the main reason why they were historically known as the exempt provinces.

At that time, fighting national emergencies forced a greater degree of fiscal effort on the people. Nevertheless, early modern governments financed extraordinary expenses, such as wars, with loans rather than taxes.[8]

During the Confederation, taxation was not a tool open to the American Congress, which instead had to rely on the state governments to tax the American people on its behalf. The period between Yorktown and the Philadelphia convention showed that this arrangement would not produce the necessary means to cover government expenditures.

In a similar way, starting in the seventeenth century but mostly during the eighteenth century, the contributions of the Basque provinces to the King of Castile were not enough to cover the expenses of the kingdom. In addition to the said taxes, the Basque provinces were obliged to make some extraordinary contributions to the lord. We can distinguish between the extraordinary payments within the foral system, by virtue of the New Law, and the extraordinary payments outside such legal framework.

Extraordinary payments within the foral system were rarely demanded by the King until the seventeenth century. One was the military service in wartime, which frequently was substituted by an amount of money large enough as to compensate for the absence of Basque men in the fighting. The other one was the money given to the Crown in order to defray the construction of roads, which was one of the main responsibilities of the foral territories.

The other kind of extraordinary payments were the gifts, extraordinary and voluntary contributions, which were required during national emergencies (like wars) by the lord. Despite the fact that they were not laid out in the New Law, the Basque provinces were not exempted from such requirements. Actually the requisitions became almost ordinary as the result of the numerous and continuous conflicts of those centuries.

---

8   The British government financed British involvement in the War of Independence by increasing its national debt by 58 million pounds. Similarly, the cost of the French participation in the conflict added almost a billion livres to France's public debts.

In the eighteenth century, fiscal pressure of the Basque provinces increased spectacularly due to these extraordinary payments deriving from wars and from the maintenance of roads. For instance, the extraordinary gifts for war were seven times higher in 1814 than in 1713, and services for the army went up from 4,200 to 17,500 over the same time period.[9]

Considering all the above, one may conclude that similar deficiencies in both American and Basque initial tax structures can be observed. First of all, both were based on requisitions or calls either to the states or—to a lesser extent, as there was a permanent income deriving from the ordinary taxes—to the Basque provinces. The voluntary nature of the payment of such requisitions prevented either the Confederation or the king from obtaining enough income to fund the increasing expense.

In the American case, for instance, Congress's six requisitions between 1781 and 1787 netted one third of what the national government has asked the states to contribute. The real problem, however, was that the returns on the requisitions decreased rapidly during the period. It went down from two thirds of the requisitions in 1781 to a mere 2 percent of the requisition in 1786.[10]

In the Basque case, although the payment was not binding, figures show that Basque provinces paid, after the required negotiation, the royal requisitions without strong opposition. According to Isabel Mugartegui, in Gipuzkoa 261 million of *maravedies* were paid to the royal treasury from 1600 to 1814.[11]

In sum, neither tax structure could provide enough income to cover the main expenditures of the time and those in power tried to increase such income by virtue of extraordinary payments, demonstrating structural deficiencies in both cases.

Closely linked to the need to enhance fiscal pressure, people's reaction to new taxes must be noted. Both the American and the Basque people

---

9   Luis María Bilbao, "La Fiscalidad en las provincias exentas de Vizcaya y Guipúzcoa durante el siglo XVIII," in *Estudios de Hacienda. De Ensenada a Mon*, ed. Miguel Artola and Luis María Bilbao (Madrid: Instituto de Estudios Fiscales, 1984), at http://conciertoeconomico.org.

10   Max M. Edling, *A Revolution in Favor of Government: Origins of the US Constitution and the Making of the American State* (Oxford: Oxford University Press, 2003).

11   Isabel Mugartegui, "La exención fiscal de los territorios forales vasco: el caso guipuzcoano en los siglos XVII y XVIII," in *Haciendas Forales y Hacienda real. Homenaje a Don Miguel Artola y Don Felipe Ruiz Martin*, ed. Emiliano Fernández de Pinedo (Bilbao: Universidad del País Vasco-Euskal Herriko Unibertsitatea, 1990).

reacted violently against the requests to pay new duties. Besides, in most cases their refusal to make these new payments was legally grounded.

In America, the colonists argued that only their own elective colonial assemblies could tax them and that the British parliament was not authorized to impose taxes on them. The defeat of Stamp Act, the Townshend Act, and, finally, the Tea Act in 1773 by the colonists' protests and revolts are good examples.

The states' reluctance reemerged clearly during the Confederation Union. The first proposal was the impost of 1781. It gave Congress the right to levy a 5 percent impost to income, which was to be used toward paying the interest and the principal of the national public debt. Because the Articles of Confederation could only be amended by unanimous ratification, the impost of 1781 was killed when Rhode Island refused to ratify it and Virginia repealed its earlier ratification. The impost of 1783 granted Congress the right to levy a 5 percent *ad valorem* duty on all imports, in addition to specified duties on certain articles. To make the amendment less objectionable to states' rights protectors, the proposal limited the grants to a twenty-five-year period. This time it was New York that denied ratification.

On the Old Continent, popular revolts in late Middle Ages were uprisings and rebellions by peasants in the countryside, or the bourgeoisie in towns, against nobles, abbots, and kings, and a part of a larger "Crisis of the late Middle Ages." Although sometimes known as peasant revolts, the phenomenon of popular uprisings was of broad scope and not just restricted to peasants. There were five main reasons for these mass uprisings: first, an increasing gap between the wealthy and poor; second, declining incomes of the poor; third, rising inflation and taxation; fourth, the external crises of famine, plague, and war; and last, religious backlashes.

In the Basque territories things were not different, taxation being one of the main causes of these revolts. In addition, the attempts to minimize the tax autonomy of the foral territories by the political reforms implemented by the Austrians and the Bourbons dynasties aiming at standardization and centralization kept the rebellion movement in these territories alive during the eighteenth century.

COMMON TRENDS IN THE EVOLUTION OF BOTH TAX STRUCTURES

American and Basque tax structures evolved mainly during the eighteenth century. The approaches of both processes lead us to identify two common trends in the evolution of their tax structures. On the one hand, the different means of financing the debts caused by war were a common issue, in both cases closely connected with tax structures. On the other, the migration from a tax structure heavily based on direct taxes (poll tax or capitations, land tax, and so on) to another whose income derived mainly from indirect taxes (excise, customs, sales, and so forth) was also a common feature of both systems.

THE AMERICAN TAX SYSTEM

Despite the dispute over taxation that went on in New England after 1763, an overall unity of theory and practice marked the taxes in the region. All the New England colonies relied on property taxes as a regular source of income. All were nominally committed to the idea that taxation ought to be related to ability to pay and that property variously defined was an acceptable measure of such ability.

However, the approach to taxation in the middle colonies differed from New England. Despite the lack of standardization among the middle colonies´ tax systems, an important unifying principle, implicit rather than avowed, did underlie many middle colonies tax systems: the interest of the landed wealthy should be protected whenever politically possible. However, no two middle colonies administered property taxes in the same way, according to exactly the same items. Taking Pennsylvania as an example of a middle colony, let us present some figures. In 1763, the amount of income from Pennsylvania Property tax was 21,235 sterling pounds, while the income from the Excise Tax was 4,002 sterling pounds. Pennsylvania property tax raised an average of 22,000 sterling pounds during the decade preceding independence. During the same decade income from excise increased remarkably, providing over 8,000 sterling pounds, while income from property taxes remained constant.[12]

---

12   Robert A. Becker, *Revolution, Reform and the Politics of American Taxation, 1763–1783* (Baton Rouge: Louisiana State University Press, 1980). See tables 8 and 9 in the appendix.

However, the huge diversity of taxes in the colonies of the South had an underlying uniformity as well. Tax laws discriminated against the politically powerless and the poor and favored the interest of men of established landed wealth, who normally dominated the southern legislatures. North Carolina is a good example to understand the common pattern: nearly three quarters of the colony´s revenues were collected by poll taxes levied on every white male aged sixteen or older and on all black people, slave or free, male or female, over the age of twelve. In effect, the poll tax on slaves operated as a property tax paid by the tax owners; otherwise, lands and commercial wealth in North Carolina escaped virtually untapped.

After the Declaration of Independence in July 1776, the new United States had to find sufficiently quickly funds to establish its independence. Although each state was unique and responded to the problems of revolutionary finance in its own way, several trends emerged, more clearly in some states than in other, but trends that were on the whole common to all of them. First, the rebel legislatures found that by declaring independence they had not escaped the conflicts over taxation that marked the late colonial years. Second, the war created new problems for all legislatures as well as new rivalries and interest groups, complicating the search for equitable and efficient tax systems. Third, the rebel governments in all sections soon faced widespread popular opposition to tax collection, even at times violent protest. As a result, the legislatures tolerated inefficiency and evasion in tax collections that seriously weaken their ability to raise money, soldiers, and supplies. And finally, there were in most states during the war movements that sought to bring under taxation income, property, and wealth that had previously gone undertaxed and to reduce or eliminate taxes popularly thought to be unfair and discriminatory against the poor and the many as opposed to the rich and the few. However, not all attempts at reform were successful, and not all were permanent.

In the end, the reason why the states exerted such heavy pressure on the citizens was because money was needed to pay interest and installments on the public debts run up by Congress and the states during the war of independence. According to some researchers,[13] 90 percent of taxes levied in the postwar years were earmarked for debt payment.

---

13   M. D. Kaplanoff, "The Hamiltonian Moment," quoted in Edling, *A Revolution in Favor of Government.*

In the debate over ratification of the American Constitution, it was often claimed that oppressive taxation arose from the mode by which a tax was raised rather than from the amount of money levied. Actually, what they were mainly concerned with was whether the taxes levied were direct or indirect. In late eighteenth century, in Britain, indirect taxes in the form of the impost, that is, custom duties and the excises, contributed about four fifths of the total revenues. The American economy, however, ensured that yields from excises would be insignificant. Due to protectionism, industrialists and merchants were very low taxed. In mainly agricultural America, the most important taxes by far were direct taxes. These took two basic forms: the land tax and the tax on polls. The main problem with these direct taxes was that they hit the lower and middle ranks relatively more than those who were better off. In fact, the poll tax, which was much used in New England, was levied at a flat rate regardless of income. Meanwhile, the land tax tended not to discriminate sufficiently between lands of various degrees of productivity.

Once the Constitution was adopted and the Federalists were in power, they came to pursue policies and create institutions consistent with the principles they had expressed in the ratification debate. The nation they made was financed almost exclusively by the revenue from customs duties.

THE BASQUE TAX SYSTEM

As mentioned before, during the eighteenth century fiscal pressure increased remarkably in the Basque territory. Up to that moment, the income deriving from the ordinary contributions of the known as exempted provinces remained constant, being increased exclusively by the king extraordinary petitions as to fund some financial emergencies. In the eighteenth century requisition by the Crown became ordinary in the sense that they were more and more frequent. The main reason for that was the continuous war conflicts in which the Spanish Crown was involved. The French Convention (1793–1796) and the Peninsular War (1808–1814), along with conflicts with the English Crown, were the most outstanding and expensive episodes. As a result, the Crown continued demanding extraordinary income and an increase in army services from the Basque provinces. Road construction was another factor with special impact on the rise of fiscal pressure in these territories.

According to data,[14] extraordinary payments in cash to the Crown went up from 1,300,000 *reales* in the period 1700–1713 to 8,050,000 *reales* in the period 1793–1814.

The increase of fiscal pressure required a change in the composition and administration of the tax system and an abandonment of direct taxation in favor of indirect taxation, and the provincial councils (*Juntas provinciales*) started to play the main role in the administration of tax systems.

In former periods, the *Juntas provinciales* were in charge of expenditure, but they had no competence to impose taxes. Taxes, mainly capitations or poll taxes (*fogueraciones*) were imposed and collected by the municipalities and the *Juntas provinciales* were mere intermediaries between municipalities and the Crown in order to pay the ordinary contributions. However, tax structures were complex and differed for each municipality. The *Juntas* were in charge of fixing the total amount of expenditure and assigning it to municipalities. Municipalities funded their assignments for provincial expenditure and their own expenditure with their common funds, deriving from capitations or consumption duties. In case the income was not enough to pay for the amounts, neighbors were required to pay extra individual revenue. Municipalities were quite free to design their tax structure, and therefore, diverse models could be found. However, during the seventeenth century rural areas' tax income was mainly based on poll taxes, while commercial municipalities' (*villas*) tax income was based on consumption.

The royal demand for extraordinary payments or gifts from the Basque provinces brought new competences to the *Juntas provinciales*, and at the beginning of the eighteenth century they were able to impose duties on red and white wine.

At the same time, the poll system started to be questioned, due to its inequity effects and the lack of certainty of the existing census, and a migration to tax structures based on consumption duties was initiated. For instance, in the 1736–1738 accounts of the Lordship of Bizkaia poll taxes were 147,764 *reales* out of a total income of 234,602 *reales* while in the 1800–1802 accounts, out of a total income of 913,115 *reales*, with just 140,234 derived from poll-taxes or *fogueraciones*.[15]

---

14 Bilbao, "La Fiscalidad en las provincias exentas de Vizcaya y Guipúzcoa."
15 Pablo Alzola, *Régimen administrativo antiguo y moderno de Vizcaya y Guipúzcoa* (1910), Clásicos de la Hacienda Foral, no. 7 (Bilbao: Diputación Foral de Bizkaia, 2009), at http://conciertoeconomico.org.

Nevertheless, this progressive change toward indirect taxation was altered due to the enormous expenses caused by wars. More income was needed in order to fund war expenses, and taxes and duties of every nature were imposed. Even a tax structure based mainly on direct taxes was re-implemented in the Basque provinces during the French occupation. In 1804, the collection of the capitations stopped, as they were no longer a good financing source.

A COMPARATIVE APPROACH

One of the challenges of comparative approaches in the field of federalism is the lack of consensus over the structure of an ideal federal system. It is clear that fiscal federalism remains a work in progress in the twenty-first century and that the ultimate fiscal structures the different federal tax models have in place are becoming blurred, in particular after the 2008 global crisis.

The 1978 Spanish Constitution establishes a vertical distribution of powers among three different levels: the federal or state level, the sub-federal or autonomous community level, and the local or municipality level.

Tax competence is horizontally distributed into five tax different systems. On the one hand, the four foral ones—one in each of the Basque provinces (Bizkaia, Araba, and Gipuzkoa) within the Basque Autonomous Community and the other in Navarre—and the state system, with its variations among the fifteen autonomous communities and the particularities of the Canary Islands and the cities of Ceuta and Melilla.

According to fiscal and financial parameters of the fiscal federalism theory, the Spanish decentralization system described above is an asymmetric federal model. The coexistence of two fiscal and financial models at the sub-federal level, the common system and the foral system, grounded on different principles and fundamentals, is the reason for this consideration. In fact, fifteen autonomous communities are within the framework of the common system and just two of them, Navarre and the Basque Country, are within the foral system. The main difference between both systems is the overwhelming tax and financial power of the foral territories, which confers them a higher degree of financial autonomy. In addition, one should not forget that the Spanish state and, consequently, the Basque foral tax systems, are within a wider federal legal framework, the European Union. The European Union legal framework undoubtedly has a say in a comparative approach between the fundamentals of the US tax system and the Basque tax system.

On the contrary, the US federal tax model is symmetrical, conferring on all the states the same tax powers subject to the same limitations by virtue of the 1789 Constitutional framework.

The European Union and the United States are both federal systems, and along with any other federal systems in the world today, face difficult choices to achieve the optimum way to distribute the various kinds of powers between the federal and sub-federal level. Competence distribution naturally leads to conflicts between different authorities. In recent decades, the battle over tax competences among different tax jurisdictions is permanently increasing. If the struggle occurs within federal frameworks, it has an added layer of complexity because of the existence of at least two constitutionally established tiers of government, each with its powers, responsibilities, and perspectives. The more decentralized fiscal power is in a federation, the more autonomy the sub-federal units enjoy in order to carry out their responsibilities. Therefore, the distribution of tax powers becomes one of the more studied and controversial aspects of federalism.

The EU and US systems belong to two different legal worlds: common law and civil law. Notwithstanding, the role of courts, outstanding in common law tradition, also has great relevance with regard to tax issues from the EU perspectives, given the inexistence of a common tax system at the federal level, since tax power remains in the sovereignty of each state and the EU budget is mainly financed by funds transferred by member states. Courts also carry out a primordially negative role in taxation in order to guarantee the fundamental freedoms and the achievement of the correct functioning of the internal market, the main objective of the Treaty of Functioning of the European Union.

The aim of this section is to compare the principles and fundamentals of the tax power distribution in the US tax system and the complex legal framework affecting the tax powers of the Basque provinces. Thus, in the twenty-first century, Basque fiscal powers are subject to three different legal orders: the European Union, the Spanish state, and the Autonomous Community of the Basque Country.

THE BASQUE TAX SYSTEM LEGAL FRAMEWORK: A GENERAL OVERVIEW

The 1978 Spanish Constitution establishes the pillars for restoring the foral traditional tax and expenditure autonomy of the foral provinces.

The Constitution, in the First Additional Provision, establishes that: "The Constitution protects and respects the historical rights of the territories with traditional Fueros. The general updating of historic rights shall be carried out, where appropriate, within the framework of the Constitution and of the Statutes of Autonomy." This provision constitutes the constitutional legal framework for the foral model in the Basque Country and Navarre and, indirectly, the recognition of the federal asymmetric model in regard to tax and financial competences.

Following the historical tradition of Economic Agreements, the update of the Basque territories' historical rights was carried out by the Statute of Autonomy of the Basque Country (known as the Statute of Gernika) approved by 2/1979 Organic Law, which in Article 41, clause 1, establishes that: "Tax relations between the state and the Basque Country shall be regulated by the traditional system of the Economic Agreement or Conventions."

The first Economic Agreement in force was that approved by the 12/1981 Law, May 13, and expired on December 31, 2001. The Economic Agreement in force for an indefinite term was approved by the 12/2002, Law, May 23.

The Economic Agreement, is based on two pillars:

    a) Fiscal Autonomy. The main taxes belong to the Basque foral provinces, also known as Historical Territories. They have the power to maintain, establish, and regulate their taxation system. The respective provincial governments have the power for the levying, administration, settlement, inspection, revision, and collection of the taxes and duties comprising their taxation system.

    b) Payment of a Quota. The Basque Autonomous Community pays the central government a certain amount of money—known as the Quota—as compensation for the expenditures made by the state on competences not transferred to the Basque region. Even though the tax power belongs to the Historical Territories, the Quota is legally assigned to the Basque Autonomous Community universally. Each territory pays a share of the Quota depending on its relative GDP and tax collection efficiency.

The result of this institutional structure is a federal model structured in four levels of government with spending powers in the Basque Country: central government, the Basque regional government, Basque provincial governments, and Basque municipalities. However, basically only one of them, that at the provincial level, is granted tax powers.[16] This leads to a complex scheme of transfers that redistributes taxes from the provincial governments toward the other tiers of government. Obviously, the European Union is the fifth level of government in the Basque Country.

In contrast to the US constitutional framework, in the case of the Basque Country, there is quite a well-structured set of rules establishing the financial and tax powers distribution between the central state and the Basque Autonomous Community and the foral territories. While it is true that there is just one provision in the 1978 Constitution that refers to historical rights in general terms, the Statute of Autonomy, the Economic Agreement, and the Historical Territories Law[17] clearly establish the distribution of tax and financial powers and the relations among the four abovementioned levels of government. These set of laws are regarded as "the constitutional legal block" by the jurisprudence of the Spanish Constitutional Court.

In the following section, an analysis of the configuration of the principles and fundamentals in both systems is presented.

FUNDAMENTALS AND PRINCIPLES
DUAL SOVEREIGNTY

Dual sovereignty is one of the main rationales for tax power distribution in both the US federal model and the Basque model.

In the case of the US tax system, the distribution of tax powers is clearly inspired by the principle of dual sovereignty as derived from

---

16   The municipalities collect some taxes, but their collection is only a small percentage of all the taxes collected in the Basque Country. The municipal taxes represent around 20 percent of the municipal revenues. The Social Security (which is under the control of the central government) also collects contributions that are used to finance pensions and unemployment benefits.

17   The 27/83 Law, November 25 .

diverse articles of the constitutional text and their interpretation by the courts. A horizontal and vertical distribution of tax powers can be distinctively observed.

As a consequence of being a previous confederation, the US constitution vertical distribution of powers between the Union and the states is based on a cession of a certain degree of tax sovereignty to the federal level strictly limited to the achievement of the competences of the Union. Paying debts, providing defense, and general welfare, as well as regulating interstate commerce, are exclusive competences assigned to the federal level. The Necessary and Proper Clause reinforces this idea. As a result, Congress can finance its expenses by imposing any kind of tax. There is not a distribution of tax powers by virtue of the nature of the different tax figures with the only exception of imports, which are of the exclusive competence of the federal level. In contrast to the Basque case, there is no distribution of tax powers depending on mutually exclusive scopes. Therefore, the federal tax system's territorial scope is the whole of the US territory and the personal scope for corporations requires them to be based in the United States. In the case of individuals, the US tax system has one of the broadest personal scopes in Comparative Tax Law and affects all US citizens and resident aliens, regardless of where they reside.

The horizontal distribution of tax power among states is prior and original, not conferred by the Constitution, and it is reinforced by the Tenth Amendment to the US Constitution. It is one of the main elements of their sovereignty based on the principles of territoriality and residence and self-limited by the cession to the federal level and by the constitutional limitations. All the states have equal capability to tax in order to finance their competences, regardless the different execution of such capability, which leads in practice to a scenario of diverse tax systems by virtue of the constitution of each state.

In the Spanish constitution, it is clearly established for the autonomous communities under the common system that the primary power to raise taxes is vested exclusively in the central state by means of law.[18] In stark contrast, in the case of the Basque tax system, the distribution of tax power is grounded on the principle of dual sovereignty. However, in comparison to US legal framework, this construct is hazier and requires a constitutional interpretation to be clearly established.

---

18   See Article 133, clause 1 of the 1978 Spanish Constitution.

The Fist Additional Provision of the 1978 Spanish Constitution acknowledges the existence of historical rights previous to the constitutional text, as in the case of the United States, and guarantees its protection and respect. As it has been commented, financial and tax capacity is one of the most outstanding foral rights and it dates back to the Old Law of Bizkaia.

However, the constitutionalization of historical rights is a novelty brought about by the 1978 Constitution into the Spanish constitutional system. In fact, this is the way to solve permanently the foral historical rights issue. In this regard, these rights are introduced in the constitutional framework and are subject to update within the constitutional text and the Statute of Autonomy.

The Constitutional Court[19] has also made a clear distinction between the origin of the powers of the foral provinces (the Historical Territories) and of the powers of the autonomous communities. The Court states that the foral territories are entitled to the historical rights subject to updating and guaranteed by the First Additional Provision of the Constitution. Therefore, in order to set out the delimitation of the powers of these territories, a historical research on which these historical rights are should be conducted.

The autonomous communities, however, are a new sub-federal level established by the 1978 Constitution, and their powers are those assumed in their statutes of autonomy within the constitutional framework. As a result, in the words of the Constitutional Court,[20] the three Basque Historical Territories were already entitled a foral self-government regime, and the Basque Statute of Autonomy legally established the Basque Autonomous Community, which gathered them in a common territorial and administrative structure.

Together with the foral institutions—the General Assemblies (Juntas Generales) and foral governments (*diputaciones*)—the system of Economic Agreements, which was historically the particular financial and tax regimen of the foral provinces, is clearly one of the historical rights that makes up the "intangible core of *forality*," as the Constitutional Court defines the essence of the powers of the foral territories.[21]

---

19 Constitutional Court Sentence 11/1984, February 2.
20 Constitutional Court Sentence 76/1988, April 26.
21 Constitutional Court Sentence 76/1988, April 26.

The fact that the Economic Agreement in Araba, unlike in Bizkaia and Gipuzkoa, was not abolished during Francoism made its restoration easier than in the case of some other historical rights. In this regard, the Eighth Transitory Provision of the Basque Statute of Autonomy states:

> Eighth. The first Economic Agreement to be concluded after the approval of this Statute shall draw its inspiration from the material contents of the current Economic Agreement with the province of Alava, without this implying any detriment to the province. State taxation on alcohol shall not be agreed upon therein.

Concurrent Powers versus Exclusive Powers

The principle of dual sovereignty, a pillar in both federal systems, leads, however, to two different kinds of relations between the federal level and the sub-federal units.

In the case of the United States, the power to tax is a concurrent power of the federal government and the individual states. Its rationale is dual sovereignty. In *Federalist Paper* Number 46 James Madison analyses this concept,[22] stressing that the federal and state governments are not adversaries or enemies but: "different agents and trustees of the people, constituted with different powers, and designed for different purposes." He articulates that they are separate yet can collaborate and that the power lies in the people. The natural attachment of the people will always be to the governments of their respective states, so the federal government must be, in a sense, extraordinarily effective to be respected.

In the early case of *Sturges v. Crowninshield* (1819), Chief Justice Marshall, in reference to the matter of bankruptcy, laid down the distinction between the exclusive and concurrent powers of the federal government, in the following language:

> When the American people created a national legislature, with certain enumerated powers, it was neither necessary nor proper to define the powers retained by the States. These pow-

---

22 The *Federalist Papers* is a collection of eighty-five letters written (under the pseudonym of Publius) by Alexander Hamilton, James Madison, and John Jay to New York newspapers in 1787 and 1788 in support of the Constitution during the debate over its ratification.

ers proceed, not from the people of America, but from the people of the several States; and remain, after the adoption of the Constitution, what they were before, except so far as they may be abridged by that instrument. In some instances, as in making treaties, we find an express prohibition; and this shows the sense of the convention to have been that the mere grant of a power to Congress did not imply a prohibition on the States to exercise the same power. But it has never been supposed that this concurrent power of legislation extended to every possible case in which its exercise by the States has not been expressly prohibited. The confusion resulting from such a practice would be endless. The principle laid down by the counsel for the plaintiff, in this respect, is undoubtedly correct. Whenever the terms in which a power is granted by Congress, or the nature of the power required that it should be exercised exclusively by Congress, the subject is as completely taken from the state legislatures as if they had been expressly forbidden to act on it.

In *Houston v. Moore* (1820), Justice Johnson says:

> The Constitution containing a grant of powers in many instances similar to those already existing in the state governments, and some of those being of vital importance also to state authority and state legislation, it is not to be admitted that the mere grant of such powers in affirmative terms to Congress, does, per se, transfer an exclusive sovereignty on such subjects to the latter. On the contrary, a reasonable interpretation of that instrument necessarily leads to the conclusion that the powers so granted are never exclusive of similar powers existing in the States, unless where the Constitution has expressly, in terms, given an exclusive power to Congress, or the exercise of a like power is prohibited to the States, or there is a direct repugnancy or incompatibility in the exercise of it by the States.

It can be concluded that the principle of concurrence of powers is the main fundamental for the distribution of powers in the US system, the principle of exclusive powers being much more restricted. In regard to finance and taxation, examples of the exclusive power of the federal government are the prohibition of any state to coin money or emit bills of credit and the exclusive competence of the federal government to tax imports.

In regard to the Basque Country, the 1978 Spanish Constitution lays out the distribution of powers between the central state and the autonomous communities. In particular, article 148 sets out the powers devolved to self-governing communities, which are included and regulated in the different statutes of autonomy, and article 149 establishes the scope within which the central state has exclusive competence. However, many of the exclusive competences of the central state in article 149 are outlined in such a way that they become concurrent powers between the central state and the autonomous communities.[23] Thus, in general terms, the principle of concurrence of powers also strongly guides the distribution of powers in the Spanish Constitution. Nevertheless, many fundamental powers are exclusive to the central state.

The Spanish Constitution also includes one clause that recalls the US doctrine of the enumerated powers and the Tenth Amendment to the US Constitution. The first part of clause 3 in article 149 states: "Matters not expressly assigned to the state by this Constitution may fall under the jurisdiction of the self-governing communities by virtue of their statutes of autonomy."

Additionally, a Supremacy Clause can be found in the second part of clause 3, which reads as follows:

> Jurisdiction on matters not claimed by statutes of autonomy shall fall with the state, whose laws shall prevail, in case of conflict, over those of the self-governing communities regarding all matters in which exclusive jurisdiction has not been conferred upon the latter. State law shall in any case be suppletory of that of the self-governing communities.

In regard to financial powers, the Constitution assigns several relevant powers exclusively to the central state, including customs and tariff regulations, foreign, monetary system, foreign currency, exchange, and convertibility, bases for the regulations concerning credit, and banking and insurance.

As mentioned before, in the case of the autonomous communities under the common regime the primary power to raise taxes is vested

---

23   Out of the thirty-two competences listed as exclusive in article 149, clause 1, the Spanish Constitution confers some power in relation to eleven additional scopes.

exclusively in the state by means of law. However, the autonomous communities and municipalities are able to impose and levy taxes, in accordance with the constitution and the laws.

The resources of the autonomous communities under the common regime in order to pay for the public services of their competence are laid out in article 157 of the Constitution, and they mainly include: taxes wholly or partially made over to them by the state,[24] surcharges on state taxes and other shares in state revenue; and their own taxes, rates, and special levies and transfers from an inter-territorial compensation fund and other allocations to be charged to the state budget.

In a similar way to the territorial conception of the state's jurisdiction in the US Constitution that ensures state taxation is confined within a state's borders, clause 2 in article 157 of the Constitution forbids the autonomous communities from introducing measures to raise taxes on property located outside their territory or likely to hinder the free movement of goods or services.

Consequently, the state holds the exclusive power to raise taxes but the Constitution also assigns to the autonomous communities the capability to have a concurrent power, subject to some limitations, with the central states with regard to the transferred taxes, and to impose taxes different from those of the central state.

Quite the contrary, in the case of the Basque Country the principle of mutually exclusive power is the one on which the distribution of the financial and tax powers is grounded, leaving a narrow scope for the principle of concurrence.

Nothing is established specifically in the Constitution about the distribution of tax and financial powers between the Basque Country and the central state. The First Additional Provision alone guarantees the historical rights, among which we find tax and financial powers, and refers its update to the statutory legal framework with respect of the constitutional principles.

In this regard, it is in article 41 of the Basque Statute of Autonomy in which the principles and guidelines for the tax relations between the state and the Basque Country are established.

---

24 See 8/1980, LOFCA (Organic Law on Financing the Autonomous
    Communities), September 22.

First, in article 41, paragraph 2a plenary legislative powers, subject to certain limitations, are assigned to the Basque Historical Territories in order to maintain, establish, and regulate the tax system within their own territory. In addition, plenary executive powers are also conferred on them for the levying, management, demand, collection, and inspection of all taxes, except for customs duties, which are under the exclusive competence of the state. Thus, the foral tax powers are complete powers in their own scope.

The result of this distribution of tax powers is the existence of two mutually exclusive tax systems. Therefore, by virtue of the Economic Agreement, the institutions of the Basque Historical Territories are equal to the institutions of the state, each in regard to the taxes and taxpayers under their scope of competence.

The Economic Agreement acknowledges this in article 1, paragraph three, when stating that for the administration, inspection, revision, and collection of the taxes within the Basque tax system, the competent institutions of the Historical Territories shall enjoy the same powers and prerogatives as those enjoyed by the state treasury.

THE UNIFORMITY CLAUSE:
A DIFFERENT SCOPE WITH A COMMON TARGET

In the Economic Agreement, there is no express uniformity clause like that in the US Constitution. However, the uniformity principle is one of the strongest limitations on the foral territories' tax powers.

One of the constitutional limits in the US constitution to federal tax power is the Uniformity Clause, article 1, section 8, clause 1, which seeks to prevent geographical discrimination that would give one state or region a competitive advantage or disadvantage in its commercial relations with the others.

In the Basque case, for each of the agreed taxes, the Economic Agreement establishes the criteria by virtue of which the legislative, inspection, and levying competences are distributed. In addition, the Economic Agreement sets the rules required to distribute the competences concerning specific formal or material issues in relation to each tax figure. As a result, the Economic Agreement regime guarantees a comprehensive tax system, with the exception of the competences the agreement confers exclusively on the state.

In general, the power of the foral territories to regulate direct taxation in their tax systems is really ample and subject to very few limitations. Quite the contrary, by virtue of the Economic Agreement, the foral territories have no power to regulate tax figures in indirect taxation and, as a result, uniformity of legislation between the Basque tax system and the state system is the rule in this scope. The main reason for this distinction is the lack of sovereignty of members states within the European Union imposed by article 113 of the Treaty of the Functioning of the European Union, preventing the interference of indirect taxation in the smooth functioning of the internal market. As in the US case, commercial relations are also the grounds for uniformity.

Therefore, in the case of the Basque tax system, when analyzing uniformity we are clearly in the scope of indirect taxation. Quite to the contrary, the uniformity clause in the US Constitution affects the whole tax system.

In direct taxation, no uniformity is required in the Basque system, although there is a set of rules that aims to avoid great divergence among the different existing tax systems. The rationale behind these rules is based on the constitutional principles of equality, progressivity, and economic capacity on which any tax system under the Spanish constitutional framework must be based. The existence of different and mutually exclusive tax systems requires a different approach from the goal of uniformity, based, mainly, on the principles of harmonization and cooperation.

However, in the early years of the 1981 Economic Agreement, many attempts were made to impose uniformity between the regulation of the Basque tax system and the state tax system, in particular regarding the corporate tax. The Supreme Court put an end to such claims issuing an overwhelming jurisprudence.

On this point, landmark interpretations were made by the Supreme Court in 1991.[25] According to its jurisprudence, it is unsustainable to require Historical Territories to regulate tax rates or tax incentives so that they are identical to the state's. Such an obligation would turn foral legislatures into copyists and, as a result, would deny tax self-governance. Such an approach would violate clause 2 in article 41 of the Basque

---

25 Supreme Court verdict, July 19, 1991, and Supreme Court verdict, May 17, 1991.

Statute of Autonomy, which acknowledges that the foral territories have not only the power to maintain but also to establish and regulate their tax regime. The Supreme Court affirms that the power to establish implies innovation and the power to regulate implies modification. In the Court's wording, the Historical Territories' power to implement a tax system differentiated from the state's is reinforced by the coordination principle and the harmonization principle that guide the relations between the both tax systems. Consequently, the Economic Agreement contains a harmonization clause and a coordination clause.

FINAL THOUGHTS

History teaches us that fiscal powers are a key question for the construction and transformation of state models. The Spanish state of autonomies is at a crucial juncture at the moment. The 1978 constitutional decentralization model shows signs of exhaustion, and its transformation in the near future seems unavoidable. Once again the fiscal question will be the cornerstone of such a transformation. The new model should guarantee the devolution of tax powers to the sub-central tiers of government and meet the federal principles of vertical and horizontal balance to a better extent than the one resulting from the application of the actual common territory LOFCA. Such a transformation should not imply the end of the fiscal asymmetry within the Spanish state. Quite the contrary, the tax and financial systems of the Basque Country and Navarre, based on the principles of unilateral risk, accountability, and solidarity, have proved to be quite efficient along these years.

Popular revolts for tax reasons are not exclusive to the past. Current processes of transformation are also provoking popular reactions grounded on fiscal issues. Nowadays, citizens are still concerned about the distribution of fiscal powers and demand higher levels of fiscal self-government. Fortunately, the violence of the riots in previous centuries has faded away and, in the era of high technology, claims and protests are demonstrated by virtual channels on many occasions.

The Basque Country is a good example of the relevance of fiscal powers for citizenship. In fact, according to Basque citizens the Economic Agreement scores 8.18 out of 10 as a self-government tool and 7.8 out of 10 as an effective tool to fight against crisis and to contribute to the

THE BASQUE TAX SYSTEM | 37

welfare of Basque society.[26] In the case of Catalonia, some of the most determining factors in the upward trend to support the independence movement by citizens are closely linked to the potential and foreseeable benefits for the Catalonian economy and the Catalans in a scenario of independency.

In the Spanish state, the Basque tax and financial asymmetry grounded on historical rights and protected by the 1978 Spanish Constitution gives rise to suspicion in some political and social sectors. In 2017, for the first time in the democratic era, the laws that amended the Economic Agreement and the Quota Law for the period 2017–2021 were not unanimously passed by the Spanish parliament. In particular, counter-opinions were presented by the Ciudadanos Party in the Spanish Congress accusing the Basque tax and financial model of being a privilege.

It is not easy to understand these critical voices and their arguments. The founding process of the United States proves that history penetrates into constitutionalism and determines the federal state model in force since 1789. In the Basque case, the historical roots of the model may be accepted, but the asymmetry of the model based on those roots seems to be out of line of fair play within the Spanish state. I still cannot understand why. For instance, the 1978 Spanish Constitution sets an asymmetrical model in the access to the autonomy, differentiating the fast and the slow track. The dual track system was not criticized and was peacefully implemented. Nor was the linguistic asymmetry of the Spanish state, which is constitutionally guaranteed. Why do tax issues provoke such a different reaction?

In comparative law, asymmetrical models—for instance, the Canadian or the Belgian ones—are widely respected by the international community. Asymmetrical federations have proved to be a satisfactory and efficient solution for territories craving for self-government, preventing state fragmentation. Legal asymmetry in federal models is just a reflection and a consequence of a particular reality with its own historical, economic, or linguistic characteristics. This is also applicable to symmetrical models. Can anybody imagine an asymmetrical federal model in the United States? What would be its rationale? Which historical roots would it reflect?

In my opinion, the smooth functioning of a tax and financial federal model does not depend on its symmetrical or asymmetrical nature. It actually depends on respect for the fundamentals of federalism, that is,

---

26 Survey by Gizaker for Ad Concordiam Association in 2012.

a proper vertical and horizontal balance, and on the design of effective equalization tools among the different tiers of government.

The other big pillar of the US and Basque tax models is dual sovereignty. It is my understanding that bilateral tax and financial relations between the central government and the Basque Country are grounded on this principle. Others believe sovereignty lies exclusively on the central state and its powers.

Therefore, in my view, the First Additional provision of the 1978 Spanish Constitution acknowledges the prior existence of the historical rights of the Basque territories, which might have a certain resemblance to the pre-constitutional American states, and guarantees them constitutional protection.

As is well known, the main fundamental of the Basque tax and financial system is the agreement between the central and the subnational tiers of government. Agreement is based on bilateral relations for the approval and amendment of the Economic Agreement and the Quota. Bilaterality requires unilateral capacity on both sides in order to reach agreements. As I see it, the dual sovereignty principle gives meaning and substance to bilateral tax relations between the central government and the Basque Country. Dual sovereignty is a common and characteristic principle in some federal models. However it is an exception within the current Spanish decentralized state. At the same time, I admit the weakness of this principle. Its fragility at the expense of the Basque Country has been evident on many occasions; among others, the unilateral approval of the extension of Economic Agreement by the central state in December 2001 or the lack of negotiations in order to settle quotas since 2007.

Therefore, a reinforcement of the bilateral nature of the tax and financial relations between the Basque Country and the central state in practice is necessary for a better functioning of the system.

A final idea to conclude: Despite the many differences between the Basque and US tax models, evident at first sight, a deeper analysis of the American model has led me to see parallels between, on the one hand, the federal Constitution of the United States and the constitutions of the individual states, and, on the other hand, the legal framework comprising the First Additional provision of the 1978 Constitution, the Statute of Autonomy of the Basque Country, and the Economic

Agreement, which, in my opinion, could be regarded as the financial and tax constitution of the Basque Country.

BIBLIOGRAPHY

Agirreazkuenaga, Joseba. *The Making of the Basque Question*. Reno: Center for Basque Studies, University of Nevada, Reno, 2011.

———, and Eduardo Alonso Olea. *The Basque Fiscal System: History, Current Status, and Future Perspectives*. Reno: Center for Basque Studies, University of Nevada, Reno, 2014.

Alzola, Pablo. *Régimen administrativo antiguo y moderno de Vizcaya y Guipúzcoa*. 1910. Clásicos de la Hacienda Foral, no. 7. Bilbao: Diputación Foral de Bizkaia, 2009. At http://conciertoeconomico.org.

Ashley, Percy. *Modern Tariff History: Germany, United States, France*. London: J. Murray, 1920.

Becker, Robert A. *Revolution, Reform and the Politics of American Taxation, 1763–1783*. Baton Rouge: Louisiana State University Press, 1980.

Bilbao, Luis María. "La Fiscalidad en las provincias exentas de Vizcaya y Guipúzcoa durante el siglo XVIII." In *Estudios de Hacienda. De Ensenada a Mon*, edited by Miguel Artola and Luis María Bilbao. Madrid: Instituto de Estudios Fiscales, 1984. At http://conciertoeconomico.org.

Edling, Max M. *A Revolution in Favor of Government: Origins of the US Constitution and the Making of the American State*. Oxford: Oxford University Press, 2003.

Monreal Zia, Gregorio. *The Old Law of Bizkaia*. Reno: Center for Basque Studies, University of Nevada, Reno, 2005.

Mugartegui, Isabel. "La exención fiscal de los territorios forales vasco: el caso guipuzcoano en los siglos XVII y XVIII." In *Haciendas Forales y Hacienda real. Homenaje a Don Miguel Artola y Don Felipe Ruiz Martin*, edited by Emiliano Fernández de Pinedo. Bilbao: Universidad del País Vasco-Euskal Herriko Unibertsitatea, 1990.

Taussig, Frank W. *State Papers and Speeches on the Tariff.* Cambridge, MA: Harvard University, 1892. At http://oll.libertyfund.org/.

————. *The Tariff History of the United States.* New York: Putnam's Sons, 1905.

Chapter 2

Economic Theories of Fiscal Federalism: The USA and the Basque Country

Nieves Pereda Chávarri

The main aim of this paper is to analyze relevant aspects of the public financial revenue system in two intergovernmental models, the Basque Country and the states of the United States, in order to assess their capacity to achieve adequate levels of autonomy of sub-central governments, efficiency, wealth distribution, equity, accountability, and so on, considering the arrangements between central and sub-central government tiers and local governments, and their capacity to overcome possible undesired effects.

There are important differences and similarities in constitutional and political framework between the two models, and this chapter considers both.

ECONOMIC THEORIES OF FISCAL FEDERALISM

Delivering quality public goods and services, in accordance with citizen preferences, solidarity principles, and efficient management principles, is the main goal of public governments, along with the promotion of economic growth. Providing these goods and services requires an expenditure model and a financial system, which take different forms across the world.

This chapter will also evaluate the different allocations of expenses and revenues in a federal system and their effects on the economy, especially the effects that arise as a result of the allocation of tax powers to different levels of government, once they are assigned spending powers.

Federal systems are formed in two different ways: by centralizing some responsibilities and by decentralizing expenses and revenues.

Examples of the centralizing process can be found in the United States, in which the original colonies decided to create a federal government, and even in the European Union, in which independent countries decided to create a new level of government, yielding some powers and competences to a higher tier. In most other cases, the decentralization allows it to be closer to the citizens' level; responsibilities allocated to the central government are granted to a sub-central or local level, to be executed by lower tiers of government.

These processes substantially affect the assignment of tax powers to different tiers of government. Decentralization is a top-down process; federalism is bottom-up: yet top-down decentralization or bottom-up centralization may require different medication for the same diagnosis.[1]

In the case of Basque Country, we find some specific features in different regions. On the one hand, the Historical Territories of Araba, Bizkaia, and Gipuzkoa joined the Spanish Kingdom, giving up some of their competences but keeping others, such as having their own financial system and self-organization competences. On the other hand, the expenditure competences are mostly given to or taken from central government through the Statute of Autonomy (Autonomy Act).

The rights of Historical Basque Territories are recognized in the current Spanish Constitution, meaning that the rights existed prior to Constitution. These rights consist mainly of having their own financial system and their own self-organizing system. Then, in relation to the Basque revenue system, we can define it as bottom-up federalism.

In the US system, federalism in also a bottom-up system. States freely decided to join the United States, ceding to the federal government some of their powers to collect taxes and to provide some public goods and services.

Even though some evidences suggests that there is a great variety of expenditure allocations among different countries, reflecting varying

---

1   Bernard Dafflon, "The Assignment of Functions to Decentralized Government: From Theory to Practice," in *Handbook of Fiscal Federalism*, ed. Ehtisham Ahmad and Giorgio Brosio (Cheltenham, UK and Northampton, MA: Edward Elgar Publishing Limited, 2006), 275.

citizen preferences, the assignments of expenditure functions to different tiers of government are more similar across nations than tax systems, which differ from one country to another.

Differences among nations in revenue functions are really important, and these differences in income systems have important effects over national and subnational economies, as this chapter explains in terms of the Basque Country and the United States.

The main question is how to finance and provide public goods in an efficient and balanced way, respecting the important issues of an economy: growth, stabilization, welfare, equality, efficiency, independence in making decisions, and avoiding any ill-effects like fiscal competence, inefficiency, and others, as well as how tax powers are run by central and sub-central governments and managed in an efficient way, with vertical and horizontal balance, with respect for solidarity, accountability, autonomy, and citizens´ preferences, and staying on a path of economic growth. These factors are becoming more and more important in a global world.

This chapter will discuss the abovementioned issues, with particular reference to the different financial systems in the Basque Country and the states of United States, focusing on taxes and their function as distribution tool and regulator of equalization, on revenue sharing, and on the role of grants.

A DESCRIPTION OF TWO DIFFERENT MODELS
THE CONSTITUTIONAL, HISTORICAL, AND POLITICAL CONTEXT

The Basque Country and Navarre are two of seventeen Spanish autonomous communities. They are two very different financial systems among the Spanish autonomous communities, so it is important to discuss them before comparing both the US and Basque models.

Two of the seventeen Spanish autonomous communities are *foral*—the Basque Country and Navarre—and the other fifteen are communities of the Common Regime, a result of the Spanish Constitution of 1978, recognized as a decentralizing process.

In the twelfth century, the current Historical Territories of Araba, Bizkaia, and Gipuzkoa (the Basque Country in this chapter), as well as Navarre, were independent "countries and kingdoms" that decided to join the Spanish Kingdom while keeping their autonomy and their rights (known as the *fueros*).

After centuries of having their own financial systems and self-organizing competences, when they were definitively integrated into Spanish Kingdom, they lost the *fueros* and they made an agreement to maintain their competencies to levy and collect taxes and other income while paying an amount to the Spanish Kingdom for public goods and services provided to the Basque people.

This pact, called the Basque Economic Agreement, is, practically, the single right reflecting their former independence that Basque people maintain today. This aspect is going to be studied later, but to summarize, it consists in levying and collecting all taxes (including personal and corporation income taxes) and in paying the Spanish state for national public services (such as defense and foreign affairs) provided to the Basque people in proportion to their percentage of the GDP.

The Basque Economic Agreement lasted from 1878 until Franco´s dictatorship. Since the Spanish Constitution recognizes the economic rights of Historical Territories, the Autonomous Communities of Basque Country and Navarre are Foral Communities, and therefore different from the rest; these are Common Regime Communities.

These issues are important, because, as regards the Common Regime Autonomies, the current Spanish federation can be defined as a top-down model, but not the Foral Regime Autonomies. Over the course of history, the Historical Territories of the Basque Country and Navarre decided to join the Spanish Kingdom while keeping all their rights. The constitution process was bottom-up, as it is in the US model, in which the colonies freely decided to unite and create the United States of America.

In Spain, the autonomous communities of the foral regime, the Basque Country and Navarre, coexist with those of the Common Regime, in which decentralization of expenditures is not as broad as previously and in which income powers are very limited, depending mainly on transfers from the central state to meet their budgetary expenditure. We find two federation models within the Spanish state, taking into account the different financial systems: bottom-up for Foral Communities, in line with pre-constitutional rights, and top-down for the other communities of the Common Regime.

In the United States, the model is bottom-up: first, states were created and had their own constitutions, and later they joined up to make the United States. Each of the fifty states has its own constitution. The power of the federal government is a delegated power from states.

The Tenth Amendment to the US Constitution says that, "The powers not delegated to the United States by the Constitution, nor prohibited by it to the States, are reserved to the States respectively, or to the people." That means it is bottom-up federalism.

These two models, of the United States and of the Basque Country respectively, share many characteristics: different levels of government, with the exercise of exclusive powers in the sub-governments, both in terms of provision of public services, with autonomy to legislate and administer, and in terms of incomes, with capacities to establish taxes in their jurisdictions. In addition, both models have constitutionally allocated powers.

A final peculiarity of the Spanish version of federalism is that Foral Communities—the Basque Country and Navarre—are, for historic reasons, subject to a separate foral regime under which they collect all taxes within their territory (except customs duties) and remit a share of them to the central government, depending upon the estimated cost of the services provided for Basque citizens by the central government.

In the United States, the allocation of expenditure and income responsibilities is defined constitutionally, while the regime of power expenses in the Basque Country is defined by its Statute of Autonomy and income competences are regulated by the Economic Agreement.

Central governments (the US federal and Spanish governments) have very similar expenses: defense, social welfare, foreign affairs, and the main legislative and judicial institutions. Both have centralized systems of social welfare and pensions, on both sides: expenses and income. The provision of public goods and services are not the subject of this chapter.

Unlike in the case of expenses, in terms of income the two sides' differences are significant. The financial resources of the Basque Country lie primarily in taxes, and it is this sub-central government that transfers funds to the central government, except for some unimportant transfers to compensate for externalities in public works or other public services.

THE BASQUE COUNTRY

The autonomy statute provides that financial relations between the state and the Basque Country shall be governed by the provisions of the Economic Agreement, a pact or agreement carried out within the scope set for it in the statute itself.

The Economic Agreement, which is a pact between Basque Country and Spanish state, is approved by a one single article law of the Spanish parliament, which means that the Spanish parliament only can vote in favor or against the previous pact, but cannot change the content of the pact, which defines the tax powers of the Historical Territories, establishing the general principles and allocating criteria with the tax regimen applicable in the rest of the (Spanish) state (the Common Regime) as well as the basis for the calculation of financial flows generated as a result of the provision of public goods by the central government for the Basque people, as well as central government revenue in relation to its correspondence with the Basque Country.

Financial and tax relations between the Basque Country and the Spanish state are based, therefore, on the Economic Agreement. It represents an agreement on each of the agreed taxes and attributes to the Basque Country not only management capacity but also tax regulation, with the limitations that result from the application of criteria for harmonization, coordination, and collaboration, as well as keeping stabilizing functions under state purview, and with the limitations contained in the allocating criteria, representing the instruments to coexist with the common system state tax; in particular in compliance with the principle of special attention to the tax structure of the state and defense of a common free market.

The Statute of Autonomy of the Basque Country, approved following the second paragraph of number two in article 151 of the Spanish Constitution, is the law that recognizes, among other issues, the competences of the Basque Country, as well as its powers, finance, and treasury.

The drawing up of the Statute of Basque Country takes into account the first additional provision of the Spanish Constitution: "The Constitution protects and respects the historic rights of the territories with traditional charters. The general updating of historic rights shall be carried out, where appropriate, within the framework of the Constitution and of the Statutes of Autonomy."

The Economic Agreement with the Basque Country, first approved by Spanish Law 12/1981 and currently enacted by the Spanish Law 12/2002, is the mainstay of the framework of the financial system in the Basque Country.

In this chapter, the Historical Territories of Araba, Bizkaia, and Gipuzkoa, are referred to as *sub-central governments* due to their special importance in the Basque Autonomous Community together with the Basque government. Note also that the competent Institutions of the Basque Country with faculties of financial supervision and regulation in matters concerning municipalities are the institutions of the Historical Territories of Araba, Bizkaia, and Gipuzkoa.

In this paper, *Sub-central authorities* refers to the Basque Country public institutions and to the institutions of the Historical Territories.

THE UNITED STATES

The US Constitution says that Congress "shall have the power to lay and collect Taxes, Duties, Impost, and Excises," but "all Duties, Impost and Excises shall be uniform throughout the United States." According to Tenth Amendment of the Constitution, "powers not delegated to the United States by the Constitution, nor prohibited by it to the States, are reserved to the States respectively, or to the people."

The Sixteenth Amendment (1913) gives Congress the power to impose and collect taxes on incomes, from whatever source derived, without apportionment among the several states, and without regard to any census or enumeration. This amendment permitted the federal government to levy and income tax on both property and labor. The constitutions of the states recognize the right of states to levy and collect taxes, with some limitations that vary widely. Thus, in United States taxes are imposed at all tiers of government.

The federal government is mainly financed by personal income taxes. The social welfare system and medicare tax income constitutes an independent fund and is imposed equally on employers and employees.

In general, sales tax and some income taxes are imposed by the states. Many state taxes were based on federal definitions. State taxes are generally treated as a deductible expense for federal tax computation.

Taxes versus Grants

The biggest difference between the financial systems of United States and of the Basque Country is the importance of grants as financial sources in the states versus their lack of importance in the Basque Country.

Intergovernmental transfers are needed in a multilevel government system, and they play a multiple role: to finance the fiscal gap, to compensate for differences in state fiscal capacities, and to exercise influence by central government on some state programs.

Most of the literature on grants concurs that transfers can have no desired effects and can be a source of inefficiencies. There is not a perfect transfer system, and in general, excluding transfers for horizontal equalization and for redistributing functions, they must be avoided as much as possible.

The Basque Country has the highest degree of revenue decentralization. Public services provided by sub-central government are financed by taxes and fees: 82 percent from taxes in 2013; with fees added in, this figure rises to 95 percent. On the other hand, in the revenue of the US states, taxes represent only 49 percent; taxes and fees together are 69 percent of total. Transfers make up 31 percent of the states' revenue.

Despite having more constitutional powers to decide their financial system, the US states actually depend more on transfers from the central government than the Basque Country does.

From the point of view of tax competences, the Basque Country could be considered a central government level instead of a sub-central tier because all the main taxes are run by this government.

On the revenue side, the central government may limit tax autonomy, that is, the ability to set tax bases and/or rates, while on the expenditure side, the central government regulation may strongly influence the sub-central government´s spending, thereby reducing discretion in setting policy.[2]

---

2   Hansjörg Blöchliger, *Decentralisation and Economic Growth Part 1: How*

SOURCES OF STATE GOVERNMENTS
REVENUE 2013

SOURCES OF BASQUE COUNTRY
REVENUE 2013

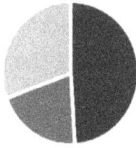

- Taxes 49%

- Fees, charges and others 20%

- Transfers 31%

- Taxes 82%

- Fees, charges and others 13%

- Transfers 5%

Sources: EUSTAT and the US Department of Commerce; Economics and Statistics Administration U.S. Census Bureau census.gov.

GRANTS

Following David N. King's model, there are some different types of grants: General grants or block grants, specific grants, and lump-sum grants or matching grants. According to King, in general the stimulus to spending is greatest where grant receipts vary according to how much effort the grantees make, either in spending on a specific service or in overall spending from taxes.[3]

Evidence shows that in the United States, sub-central spending is affected much more by changes in lump-sum grants than by equal value changes in the tax payments of grantee citizens. This phenomenon is known as the "flypaper effect."

According to Chris Edwards,[4] in the United States, the federal government has developed a highly complex financial system called the

Fiscal Federalism Affects Long-Term Development, OECD Working Papers on Fiscal Federalism No. 14 (Paris: OECD Publishing, 2013), at http://dx.doi.org/10.1787/5k4559gx1q8r-en.

3   David N. King, *Fiscal Tiers: The Economics of Multi-level Government* (1984; London: Routledge Revivals, 2016).

4   Chris Edwards, "Fiscal Federalism in the United States," in *Federalism and Fiscal Tranfers: Essays on Australia, Germany, Switzerland,and the United States*, ed. Jason Clemens and Niels Veldhuis ([Vancouver]: Fraser Institute, 2013), 31–42.

Grants-in-Aid system, which has grown progressively over a century and has affected the financing of states and local activities.

It does not seem that the intention of the founders of the American Constitution, which designed a system in which the federal government's powers were limited by the assigned functions, leaving the allocation of provisions not included in the Constitution in the hands of the states and the American people, in the Constitution's Tenth Amendment: "The powers not delegated to the United States by the Constitution, nor prohibited by it to the States, are reserved to the States respectively, or to the people."[5]

According to Jason Clemens and Niels Veldhuis, "unfortunately, policymakers and courts have mainly discarded federalism in recent decades. Congress has undertaken many activities that are traditionally reserved to the states and the private sector. The Grants-in-Aid program is a key mechanism that the federal government has used to extend its power into state and local affairs: part and parcel with these subsidies come federal regulations designed to micromanage state and local activities."[6] They recognize advantages in the system of Grants-in-Aid program, but also the disadvantages, arguing that the aid system encourages excessive spending and bureaucratic waste and a lack of political accountability, and it also stifles diversity and innovation policy in the states.[7]

Most scholars in the United States agree that improving the sub-national level of government led to reduced transfers, which creates a disincentive to improve. Some authors take a position against the grant system because the complex and often opaque nature of these transfer mechanisms.

TAXES

In any governmental fiscal system there are three critical aspects in revenue policy: tax revenue administration and revenue management, how the revenue obtained is spent, and who gets what.[8]

---

5   Jason Clemens and Niels Veldhuis, "Introduction," in *Federalism and Fiscal Tranfers*, ed. Clemens and Veldhuis, 13–16.
6   Ibid.
7   Ibid.
8   Richard M. Bird, *Fiscal Decentralization and Decentralizing Tax Administration: Different Questions, Different Answers*, GSU Paper 1509, International Center for Public Policy Working Paper Series, Andrew

The United States has a multilevel government, and each level is responsible of the administration of its own taxes. Some taxes are administrated by a higher level; for instance, local sales taxes are administered by the state in 38 states, and in most cases the state assesses the value of real property.

The Basque Country, on the other hand, is a centralized model of tax administration within a sub-central level of government (singularity), even more centralized than the autonomous communities of the Common Regime because all competences and taxes belong to Historical Territories. Local governments and the common Basque government receive transfers in a tax-sharing model, following predetermined rules to determine the amount to receive. They hardly have conditional transfers that mean the autonomy of these governments is guarantee.

ECONOMIC EFFECTS OF FINANCIAL FEATURES IN BOTH MODELS

The goal of this chapter is to provide a general idea about the economic effects of the financial systems of sub-central governments in US states and in the Basque Country.

STABILIZATION FUNCTIONS

Stabilization policies aim to maintain the economic framework under appropriate conditions to encourage growth and, above all, to avoid an economic crisis and negative consequences for the economy such as inflation, unemployment, and fiscal deficits. The most important policies are monetary policy, fiscal policy, and market regulation.

There is general consensus in accepting that sub-central authorities should not play any part in stabilization functions. The primary responsibility for macroeconomic stabilization must rest with the central government.[9]

Young School of Public Policy, Georgia State University, 2015.

9   R. A. Musgrave, "Who Should Tax, Where and What?" In *Tax Assignment in Federal Countries*, ed. Charles E. McLure, Jr. (Canberra: Centre for Research on Federal Financial Relations, Australian National University, in association with the International Seminar in Public Economics; New York: Distributed by ANU Press, 1983), 2–19.

Sub-central government budget policies can affect stabilization, especially through uncontrolled budget deficits and also through tax increases. The solution to these problems is based mainly on the establishment of strict policies to control budgetary stability and in a good harmonization of tax policies with sub-central governments.

Assuming that policies of inflation control and other monetary policies correspond to the Federal Reserve in the case of the United States and to the European Central Bank in the case of the Basque Country, it only remains to be determined how the controls of fiscal deficit and public debt, as well as tax increases, are managed in each model. Ultimate impact on fiscal discipline depends on the country's financial and political institutions.[10]

It is obvious that stabilization functions work better the bigger their jurisdiction is. It has been said that the problem in Europe is the lack of this function at the highest level, because some of the functions to achieve stabilization, such as fiscal and budgetary measures, rest with member states (France, Spain, Greece, Germany, and so on) and, on the other hand, some monetary functions only correspond to European institutions. However, the aftermath of the 2008 financial crisis brought about a crucial turning point in the EU stabilization policy.

In both models, the possibility of helping any sub-central government in order to achieve stabilization is not contemplated constitutionally or statutorily. In theory, neither the US states nor the Basque Country can be rescued by the central government.

In the United States the distinction between redistribution and stabilization is relevant to avoiding potential bailouts. Some stabilization functions could be undertaken through redistribution programs.

Grants tend to exacerbate sub-central cyclical revenue fluctuations,[11] especially in United States, where grants are really significant in financing states' expenditures and are affected by federal policies. On the other hand, this central control makes it easier to reduce deficits.

Many in the United States believe that the federal transfer program depends mainly on political decisions and is subject to political pressures;

---

10   Marianne Vigneault, "Grants and Soft Budget Constraints," in *Intergovernmental Fiscal Transfers: Principles and Practice*, ed. Robin Boadway and Anwar Shah (Washington, D.C.: The World Bank, 2007), 133–72.

11   Agnese Sacchi and Simone Salotti, "The Influence of Decentralized Taxes and Intergovernmental Grants on Local Spending Volatility," *Regional Studies* 51, no. 4 (2015), 507–22.

it is reasonable to think this possibility exists. If the transfer program is not transparent, it is difficult to assert that no possibility of hidden bailouts exists.

In conclusion, in both models, stabilization through monetary policies rests in the hands of the central government or at another superior level, such as the European Monetary Authorities, as all economic federalism theories recommend. None of them have access to central bank financing.

Fiscal deficits in sub-central governments cannot be controlled by the central government in the United States or in the Basque Country, as will be explained later.

DISTRIBUTIONS FUNCTIONS

A central government's income tax system must be focused on redistribution: the more progressive a federal tax system is, the better to reach redistribution targets across the country, and also, the bigger a country is, the better it is to redistribute among people.

It is important to consider that the most important taxes of the states, like sales and excise taxes, are very regressive. According to Carl Davis and others,[12] poor families pay almost eight times more of their incomes in these taxes than do the wealthiest families, and middle-income families pay more than four times the rate of the wealthy.

Then, a general distributive function is assigned to the central government. To get a redistributive function, progressive taxes are necessary; in other cases, redistribution is only possible through expensive social programs financed by unprogressive taxes. Then, as many of the states have sales taxes as their biggest financial resource, their role in redistribution function is very limited.

It is important to underline that in both models, the United States and the Basque Country, social welfare payments are collected by the central government. These expenditures are so important that they imply the biggest expenditure in redistribution functions.

---

12   Carl Davis, Kerry Davis, Matthew Gardner, Robert S. McIntyre, Jeff McLynch, and Alla Sapozhnikova, *Who Pays? A Distributional Analysis of the Tax Systems in All 50 States* (Washington, D.C.: Institute on Taxation and Economic Policy, 2009).

The distributive function in both models is assumed by the central government: 87.76 percent in the United States and 90.84 percent in Spain through social protection spending,[13] considering only the expenses directly related to distributive functions, and not those performed indirectly.

These data are relevant because sometimes the Basque financial model has been accused of being discordant. As most of the redistributive functions are managed by the central government, the model can be considered, in some way, as solidary. The best way to distribute wealth is through progressive taxes, whose percentage in declining in most of developed countries.

It is important to underline that redistribution programs in the United States are financed through federal funds, and that at the same time these funds are financed with direct taxes (income tax), which is very significant because redistribution in this case is made in two ways: through transfers and the direct taxes. This pattern is very uncommon in other countries.

Other ways to distribute wealth among citizens of a country is through expenses, mainly in infrastructure. These means are used by central governments: in the United States mainly through conditional transfers, and in the case of Basque Country, the central government expends on railroad and other infrastructure. This is also the case with European funds for infrastructures and others.

VERTICAL FISCAL ASYMMETRY

The conventional perspective on Vertical Fiscal Imbalance measures the imbalance between "revenue authority" and "spending responsibilities" by looking at the data on sub-national governments' revenues and expenditures.[14]

When expenditure responsibilities are taken as a given, Vertical Fiscal Asymmetry can be addressed either through a reallocation of revenue

---

13   OECD, *Fiscal Federalism 2014: Making Decentralization Work* (Paris: OECD Publishing, 2013), at http://dx.doi.org/10.1787/978926204577-en.

14   Chanchal Kumar Sharma, "Beyond Gaps and Imbalances: Re-Structuring the Debate on Intergovernmental Fiscal Relations," *Public Administration* 90 (2012), 99–128.

powers (excluding borrowing powers) or a system of intergovernmental transfers (excluding loans).

The change in revenue or in expenses has not been taken into account in any of the models examined here. It is not an option. In the United States the composition of the financial system is determined by the state constitutions and the US Constitution.

In the Basque Country, as well, the distribution of incomes among different tiers is determined by the Spanish Constitution and the Basque Economic Agreement.

In any case, in order to study Vertical Fiscal Asymmetry and its effects and consequences, is appropriate to follow theories of Vertical Fiscal Imbalance (VFI). In J. Stuart Hunter's view, a lack of subnational control over revenue sources is synonymous with VFI.[15] In his opinion, VFI affects sub-central autonomy. VFI in the two sub-central governments has very different features.

In the Basque Country, where transfers go from the bottom to the top, from sub-central government to central government, this asymmetry affects Basque autonomy only to the degree that the amount paid to the central government is determined by the expenses of the central government. The gap in relative terms is not very significant.

On the other hand, in the United States, the gap between taxes and incomes of the sub-central governments and the expenses of the services they provide is relevant: about 50 percent.

Based on econometric evidence from the United States and similarly situated countries, Jason Sorens concludes that vertical fiscal gaps incentivize bigger, more expensive, and more indebted government and inhibit the democratic accountability and responsiveness of sub-central governments.[16]

---

15 J. Stuart Hunter, *Federalism and Fiscal Balance: A Comparative Study* (Canberra: Australian National University Press and Centre for Research on Federal Financial Relations, 1977).
16 Jason Sorens, *Vertical Fiscal Gaps and Economic Performance: A Theoretical Review and an Empirical Meta-analysis*, Mercatus Working Paper (Arlington, VA: Mercatus Center at George Mason University, 2016).

EQUALIZATION

While fiscal equalization is effective in reducing tax competition and providing all jurisdictions with sufficient resources to fund public services, there is growing evidence that over time it can slow down regional convergence between rich and poor jurisdictions.[17]

Fiscal equalization means reducing the differences in revenue-raising capacity and public expenditure needs across different sub-central governments. The way to do it is with transfers.

Clearly, when it comes to equalization and solidarity it is referred to a certain citizenship within a given geographical area, in relation to a particular jurisdiction or country that has become, as a result of various factors configured in a certain way, a territory, some administrative divisions, some states (federal or centralized), a sovereign setting, which we accordingly take for granted.

Decentralization of the allocation function in public service provision enhances the efficiency of this function in the public sector,[18] but lower-level jurisdictions often have insufficient revenue capacity to meet all their expenditure needs, creating a horizontal imbalance in comparison to other sub-central economies.

On the other hand, equalization can produce perverse results. It is important to avoid value judgments about interregional fairness, solidarity, and national cohesion. According to Paul Bernd Spahn, fairness and solidarity rarely go beyond satisficing existing political claims. Yet fairness and solidarity often fall short of satisficing, because majority regions or groups are not prepared to pay a price for pacifying minorities. Not paying this price could create political uproar and secessionist tendencies.[19]

The Basque Country participates in the Interregional Solidarity Fund through the amount paid to central government, known as the Quota, and fixed according to the GDPs of the Basque Country and of Spain.

---

17 Anke S. Kessler and Christian Lessmann, *Interregional Redistribution and Regional Disparities: How Equalization Does (Not) Work*, Discussion Paper 8133 (Washington, D.C.: Center for Economic Policy Research, 2011).

18 Wallace E. Oates, "An Essay on Fiscal Federalism," *Journal of Economic Literature* 37 (September 1999), 1120–49.

19 Paul Bernd Spahn, "Equity and Efficiency Aspects of Interagency Transfers," in *Intergovernmental Fiscal Transfers*, ed. Boadway and Shah, 75–106.

Equalization is easier to achieve in the United States than in the Spanish central government, because the easiest way to do so is through transfers.

BUDGET CONSTRAINTS

"For a democracy to be consolidated, elites, organizations, and the mass public must all believe that the political system they actually have in their country is worth obeying and defending."[20]

According to OECD´s report about Fiscal Federalism in 2014,[21] sub-central consolidation is needed in the long term: governments at all levels have to respect the budget constraint whereby the present value of all future government spending must equal the present value of all future government revenues.

Where economic entities can expect their deficits to be covered is by some form of supporting organization, known as soft budget constraints. Such entities can be corporations, banks, nonprofit organizations, and even entire nations.[22]

Both models have guarantees to provide hard budget constraints. The financial and budgetary system of the Basque Country is based on a pact with Spanish state, in which autonomy means no possibility of rescue if it is in trouble. Nor can the federal states be rescued either, according to the Constitution; thus, the guarantee of a hard budget constraint is fundamental to the institutions.

In the Basque System, as a result of the compulsory agreement between the two tiers, the sub-central government cannot undermine federalism for two main reasons: the first is that it cannot modify in any case the central situation—in other words, the risk is unilateral, the Basque Country is not the recipient of any grant or transfer, and there is not any way to do that; the second is that central government has only one way of restraining the Basque Country because if the central

---

20 Larry Diamond, *Developing Democracy: Toward Consolidation* (Baltimore: Johns Hopkins University Press, 1999), 65.
21 OECD, *Fiscal Federalism 2014.*
22 János Kornai, Eric Maskin, and Gérard Roland, "Understanding the Soft Budget Constraint," *Journal of Economic Literature* 41, no. 4 (2003), 1095–1136.

government increases expenses in competences not taken on, that means that the central government should restrain itself.

The Autonomous Community of the Basque Country is one of the least indebted in per capita terms in the Spanish state; it seems to have enough discipline to maintain a viable system. Basque citizens are concerned about the sustainability of their model; thus, their hard budget constraint is very relevant in the long term.

Standard and Poor's says:

> In our view, the Basque Country's high fiscal autonomy and strong financial management make it more resilient than Spain in a sovereign stress scenario. We consequently rate the Basque Country two notches higher than Spain. We are therefore raising our long term issuer credit.
>
> The region's export oriented and competitive industry, focused on internationally diverse markets, which partly mitigates its high degree of integration with Spain's economy;
>
> Its special constitutional status, which isolates the region from negative intervention by the sovereign; Its financing system, with high fiscal autonomy that does not rely on transfers from the central government to any meaningful degree.[23]

The independence of the states in the United States, their constitutional restrictions about debt, and the impossibility of federal bailouts, closely resemble the situation in the Basque Country. On the other hand, states have very limited debt options, and when they have this option, they depend on markets, usually bond markets. Well-functioning capital markets in United States serve to punish irresponsible governments with higher borrowing costs.[24]

Transfers create a fiscal illusion and provoke increased spending. Whether or not they are for current expenditures, the reduction is very difficult once it has been established for some services or for investment. In the latter case it can be understood that investments generate an increase or improvement in the delivery of certain public services, but which in turn will keep generating the current level of expenditure.

23 Standard and Poor's, October 6, 2015.
24 Vigneault, "Grants and Soft Budget Constraints."

Unless they are designed appropriately, transfers create soft budget constraints[25] and the expectation that the federal government will "bail out" the failing subnational government.

Both models have reasons for controlling the debt, but some factors like transfers can create difficult budget constraints.

AUTONOMY

The power of central and sub-central governments lies in their economic power to raise income. From this point of view, the Basque Country has a high level of autonomy and accountability, with positive effects on stability of expenditure.

There is strong intergovernmental interdependence in the United States rather than a constitutional provision prescribing intergovernmental transfers or any constitutionally specified portions of federal taxes dedicated to be transferred to state governments.[26] The predominant pattern of transfers in the United States is a conditional transfer system.

In the United States, the large number of states and the separation of powers within both levels of government have led to a diffused, complex, and relatively uncoordinated set of financial transfers and intergovernmental relationships. At the same time, in the application of the variety of ad hoc financial arrangements, the federal government has relied extensively on conditional grants to state and local governments, and this has given relations between governments in the United States a highly complex interdependent character.[27]

In comparison to the Basque Country, and despite having more autonomy in regulating and levying taxes, the states have less autonomy in practice because they are becoming more and more dependent on federal conditional transfers.

---

25 János Kornai, "Resource-Constrained Versus Demand-Constrained Systems," *Econometrica* 47, no. 4 (1979), 801–19.
26 Robin Boadway and Ronald L. Watts, *Fiscal Federalism in Canada, the USA, and Germany*, Working Paper (Kingston, Ont.: Queen's University, 2004).
27 Ibid.

EFFICIENCY

The more detailed and closer to citizens the provision of a public service is, the more suitable it is to their preferences, the more accountable it is and, consequently, more efficiently it is provided. That is, the closer a government is to its constituents, the easier it knows how well it provides public goods, monitors expenses, accounts for revenues and expenses, and delivers public goods with a high standard of quality and low cost.

There are some opinions about efficiency at different government tiers. One is based on the inefficiency created internally when citizens cannot relate to public expenses and public incomes. Another is the inefficiency related to the administrative cost of running transfers that are monitored by a grantor.

There is another opinion concerning the increasing cost of public services when sub-central government shares expenses with central funds, which means sometimes sub-central governments are in some way obliged to finance services only because they are partly financed by central funds.

This dysfunction appears in the United States and in other developed countries. In the Basque Country, similar dysfunction can appear when a service, infrastructure, or public good is cofinanced by European funds or by other transfers, but as these funds are often for limited programs or investments, they are a way of encouraging economic growth.

ACCOUNTABILITY

The more independent the fiscal systems are from central governments, the more fiscally responsible they are. In fiscal federalism theories, accountability is one of the most important defenses of decentralization, because accountability is believed to function better in decentralized than in centralized governments.

Designing an income system in federalism must take into account some criteria so as not to undermine accountability and to be responsive to constituents' wishes. The smaller the vertical fiscal gap, the better for accountability, because each government level has to be responsible for the public services provided by its taxes.

The question is how to improve accountability when the relation between paid taxes and provided services by each of the government tiers is small because of large differences in revenue and expense decentralization.

There is a fiscal gap in the two assessed models in this chapter, which is compensated by intergovernmental transfers, from the lower level to the central government in the Basque Country and from federal government to the states in the United States.

In the Basque Country, the role of the Quota transfer to the central government is small in relation to budget amount. The fiscal gap is small, and accountability is easier. Constituents can easily perceive the provided services by sub-central government with the taxes they have paid.

In the United States the correspondence between provided services and paid taxes is more difficult. Constituents receive public services from the states that are financed by the central government. Accountability could be undermined by this factor.

On the other hand, as most of the intergovernmental transfers in the United States are conditional grants, transparency is bigger than if they were block grants, and accountability is favored by this condition.

DECENTRALIZATION AND GROWTH

The relationship between decentralization and growth is stronger for revenue decentralization than for spending decentralization, suggesting that a budget's revenue side is a better gauge for the link between fiscal frameworks and economic performance than the spending side. Decentralization is also positively linked to total factor productivity and human capital.[28]

This affirmation is positive for the Basque Country, in which the revenue system is managed by the Basque Country itself, and highlighted by the fact that all the taxes are collected by the Historical Territories, that is, at a level very close to the citizens, and by the fact that the sub-central government finances central government expenditures (in accordance with its participation in total GDP). This is not the situation of states, in which finance resources depend on federal transfers. Their decentralization is bigger on the spending side than on the revenue side.

---

28 Blöchliger, *Decentralisation and Economic Growth.*

According to Hansjörg Blöchliger's data on elasticities between output variables and decentralization indicators, revenue-side decentralization has a stronger and more significant impact than spending-side decentralization, which may reflect problems with measuring true spending autonomy. In particular, regressions over sub-periods suggest that tax autonomy has emerged as a significant driver for both GDP and productivity in the last decade.[29]

In any case, economic growth can depend on fiscal autonomy, but also on other factors that can have more impact over it, such as labor and commercial legislation, the financial system, and so on, which in the Basque Country depend on the central government.

CONCLUSION

In its formation, the Basque Country could be considered similar to the states of the United States, since its relations with the central state are similar to those of the states in the United States and can be considered as confederations in the sense that their powers are constitutionally recognized and their formation comes from a coming together federal political order, that is, the relationship between the central state and the sub-central governments comes from a desire to unite before the union: bottom-up federalism.

The relationship of the Basque Country, together with Navarre, is asymmetrical in relation to the rest of Spain's autonomous communities, which could not be defined as federalism either, but rather as decentralized governments, since decentralized authorities in unitary states (autonomous communities) can typically be revoked by central legislature at will. In fact, they are straddling the federation and the decentralized state.

Regarding the issue of this chapter, the Basque Country enjoys a system of public funding much more decentralized than that of the United States, since it collects all the main taxes, excluding social welfare contributions.

It is the Basque Country that finances the central government for the costs of the competences not assumed, based on the income of its Historical Territories, receiving subsidies from the central government in nonsignificant percentages mainly to compensate externalities. The

---

29 Ibid., 10.

Basque Country is a unique model in which the sub-central state of lower rank collects some of its income for the central state and practically self-finances.

However, in the United States the financing of sub-central governments is only 49 percent (2013 data) through taxes and 31 percent through transfers from the federal government. In the Basque Country, financing through its own taxes reaches 82 percent (also data from 2013). (See the graph in this chapter).

Therefore, although constitutionally the powers of the sub-central states of the United States are greater than those of the Basque Country, the latter enjoys much more autonomy, especially in financing, although it is more conditioned by other regulations of the central government.

The Basque Country has full autonomy to exercise its tax powers, although this is constrained by the lack of competition in civil, commercial, and labor regulations defined by the central government.

As for the two important sources of financing in both models, taxes and transfers, their composition has different effects, and the two models are conditioned by these sources.

From the economic point of view of public revenues, we can conclude the following:

- With respect to stabilization functions, recognized throughout the literature as functions that should preferably be exercised by the central government, in both models these are not assigned to the sub-centers either because they correspond to the federal government in the case of the United States or to the European Institutions or the central government in the case of the Basque Country.

- Pure redistributive functions, which finance pensions, and others are practically assigned in both models to central governments. In the United States, where the federal government incomes come mainly from direct taxes, the effect of redistribution is greater, since two important factors are added: redistribution through transfers and redistribution due to the progressivity of the income that finances them.

- Independently of the different theories on efficiency in decentralized collection, the vertical fiscal imbalance or gap is much higher in the United States than in the Basque Country. The imbalance could occur in the Basque country in positive territory; that is, it is collected more than necessary to finance the assigned competences, but the difference between income and expenses is not too important in relative terms. It can be said that in the Basque Country the vertical fiscal gap is really small: the competences assigned are financed by their own taxes.

However, in the United States, the difference is important, and it is financed by transfers from the federal government to the states.

- The budget restriction policies are effective in both models, since the response to readjustments to avoid the deficit is consistent. Both sub-central governments have strong restrictions on increasing spending through debt. In none of the systems is there the possibility of being rescued and of attacking the commons.

- In horizontal equity with other sub-central governments, although the Basque Country collaborates in the Interregional Compensation Fund, its collaboration is proportional to its income; it is not progressive, as it is in the United States, since it is affected by direct taxes.

- Fiscal autonomy, according to the constitutional system, is strong in the states of the United States, although in practice it is more widely enjoyed in the Basque Country.

BIBLIOGRAPHY

Bahl, Roy. *Intergovernmental Transfers in Developing and Transition Countries: Principles and Practice.* Washington, D.C.: The World Bank, 2000.

Bird, Richard M. *Fiscal Decentralization and Decentralizing Tax Administration: Different Questions, Different Answers.* GSU Paper 1509. International Center for Public Policy Working Paper Series. Andrew Young School of Public Policy, Georgia State University, 2015.

Blöchliger, Hansjörg. *Decentralisation and Economic Growth Part 1: How Fiscal Federalism Affects Long-Term Development.* OECD Working Papers on Fiscal Federalism No. 14. Paris: OECD Publishing, 2013. At http://dx.doi.org/10.1787/5k4559gx1q8r-en.

Boadway, Robin, and Ronald L. Watts. *Fiscal Federalism in Canada, the USA, and Germany.* Working Paper. Kingston, Ont.: Queen´s University, 2004.

Clemens, Jason, and Niels Veldhuis. "Introduction." In *Federalism and Fiscal Transfers: Essays on Australia, Germany, Switzerland and the United States,* edited by Jason Clemens and Niels Veldhuis. [Vancouver]: Fraser Institute, 2013.

Dafflon, Bernard. "The Assignment of Functions to Decentralized Government: From Theory to Practice." In *Handbook of Fiscal Federalism,* edited by Ehtisham Ahmad and Giorgio Brosio. Cheltenham, UK and Northampton, MA: Edward Elgar Publishing Limited, 2006.

Davis, Carl, Kerry Davis, Matthew Gardner, Robert S. McIntyre, Jeff McLynch, and Alla Sapozhnikova. *Who Pays? A Distributional Analysis of the Tax Systems in All 50 States.* Washington, D.C.: Institute on Taxation and Economic Policy, 2009.

Diamond, Larry. *Developing Democracy: Toward Consolidation.* Baltimore: Johns Hopkins University Press, 1999.

Edwards, Chris. "Fiscal Federalism in the United States." In *Federalism and Fiscal Transfers: Essays on Australia, Germany, Switzerland, and the United States,* edited by Jason Clemens and Niels Veldhuis. [Vancouver]: Fraser Institute, 2013.

Hunter, J. Stuart. *Federalism and Fiscal Balance: A Comparative Study.* Canberra: Australian National University Press and Centre for Research on Federal Financial Relations, 1977.

Kessler, Anke S., and Christian Lessmann. *Interregional Redistribution and Regional Disparities: How Equalization Does (Not) Work.* Discussion Paper 8133. Washington, D.C.: Center for Economic Policy Research, 2011.

King, David N. *Fiscal Tiers: The Economics of Multi-level Government.* 1984. London: Routledge Revivals, 2016.

Kornai, János. "Resource-Constrained Versus Demand-Constrained Systems." *Econometrica* 47, no. 4 (1979): 801–19.

Kornai, János, Eric Maskin, and Gérard Roland. "Understanding the Soft Budget Constraint." *Journal of Economic Literature* 41, no. 4 (2003): 1095–1136.

Musgrave, R. A. "Who Should Tax, Where and What?" In *Tax Assignment in Federal Countries,* edited by Charles E. McLure, Jr. Canberra: Centre for Research on Federal Financial Relations, Australian National University, in association with the International Seminar in Public Economics; New York: Distributed by ANU Press, 1983.

Oates, Wallace E. "An Essay on Fiscal Federalism." *Journal of Economic Literature* 37 (September 1999): 1120–49.

———. "Toward a Second-Generation Theory of Fiscal Federalism." *International Tax and Public Finances* 12 (2005): 349–73.

OECD. *Fiscal Federalism 2014: Making Decentralization Work*. Paris: OECD Publishing, 2013. At http://dx.doi.org/10.1787/978926204577-en.

Rodden, Jonathan. "Reviving Leviathan: Fiscal Federalism and the Growth of Government." *International Organization* 57, no. 4 (Fall 2003): 695–729.

Sacchi, Agnese, and Simone Salotti. "The Influence of Decentralized Taxes and Intergovernmental Grants on Local Spending Volatility." *Regional Studies* 51, no. 4 (2015): 507–22.

Sharma, Chanchal Kumar. "Beyond Gaps and Imbalances: Re-Structuring the Debate on Intergovernmental Fiscal Relations." *Public Administration* 90 (2012): 99–128.

Sorens, Jason. *Vertical Fiscal Gaps and Economic Performance: A Theoretical Review and an Empirical Meta-analysis*. Mercatus Working Paper. Arlington, VA: Mercatus Center at George Mason University, 2016.

Spahn, Paul Bernd. "Equity and Efficiency Aspects of Interagency Transfers." In *Intergovernmental Fiscal Transfers: Principles and Practice, edited*, edited by Robin Boadway and Anwar Shah. Washington, D.C.: The World Bank, 2007.

Vigneault, Marianne. "Grants and Soft Budget Constraints." In *Intergovernmental Fiscal Transfers: Principles and Practice*, edited by Robin Boadway and Anwar Shah. Washington, D.C.: The World Bank, 2007.

Weingast, Barry R. *Self-Enforcing Constitutions: With an Application to Democratic Stability in America's First Century*. Stanford: Stanford University Press, 2005.

———. "Second Generation Fiscal Federalism: The Implications of Fiscal Incentives." *Journal of Urban Economics* 65, no. 3 (2009): 279–93.

Chapter 3

Tax Harmonization in the United States Compared to the European Union and the Basque Country

Mikel Amuriza Fernandez

Although fiscal harmonization has been a topic of continuous discussion and controversy among decentralized fiscal systems since its initiation, significant progress has been made in international organizations such as the Organisation for Economic Co-operation and Development (OECD) to avoid what would fundamentally be double taxation as well as tax evasion in territories with low taxation.

However, there are various economic theories about the positive aspects of fiscal harmonization and less harmonizing fiscal policies within the international tax environment, such as the American tax system, which prioritizes tax competition over fiscal coordination and harmonization both internally and internationally.

We must also mention the globalization and internationalization of markets in continuous and growing development that consequently imply an analysis of the fiscal system in relation to continuous and rapid economic change to adapt it to the fiscal objectives that arise.[1]

Here is where you can see the difference in tax policy between the European Union, or at least the European Commission, and the US federal government and especially the current (2018) Republican government, whose fiscal policy is aimed at attracting foreign capital and substantial tax cuts.

---

1 http://www.oecd.org/tax/tax-challenges-arising-from-digitalisation-interim-report-9789264293083-en.htm.

However, as developed in this chapter, there are similar problems in other decentralized systems such as the United States and the European Union due to the political, cultural, and economic differences among the members of the United States and European Union, as well as in the Basque Country.

Therefore, this analysis will primarily compare the federal fiscal system of the United States to Europe and secondarily compare the state of Nevada to the Basque Country, because they are both decentralized at the state level.

In the first place, the decentralized tax system of the United States will be compared to the European Union, for although they may seem very different in the fiscal area, there are more similarities in tax matters than differences. This analysis will first try to analyze each system's advantages and disadvantages and later will analyze the differences with our tax system within the European Union.

The European Union and the United States are two federal systems, and like any decentralized system, they have the problem of solving on how to divide the authority and fiscal power between the central governments and the member states. This same problem exists in Spain, even though it is not a federal state, and in which different fiscal systems exist in the central government, Navarre, the Basque Country, and the other autonomous communities.

It is worth mentioning the difficulties that have occurred and are occurring in the current Economic Agreement between the Basque Country and Spain with the harmonization terms due to the non-specification of their application in the Economic Agreement Text.

The following two principles established in the Economic Agreement:[2]

1. The principle of non-distortion of competition, by which entities can move freely within Spain.

2. The effective fiscal pressure in Basque Country must be equivalent to that existing in the rest of the state.

The first principle, if interpreted restrictively, turns out to be contradictory, with the exclusive power to regulate the direct taxes that the so-called Historical Territories (the Basque provinces) have

---

2   http://www.conciertoeconomico.org/en/about-the-economic-agreement/history-of-the-agreement/historical-landmarks-of-the-agreement.

according to the Economic Agreement and that would leave without application of the same.

It is necessary to specify that indirect taxes must be regulated in an identical manner to that established by the state, that is, in a uniform manner, whereas the Historical Territories have full legislative competence with respect to direct taxes.

Therefore, direct taxes are subject to these harmonization rules that must be met, and this is where disputes arise: These forms of interpretation have been subject to numerous litigations in the corporate income tax between the Historical Territories and the central government or autonomous communities.

INTRODUCTION TO THE AMERICAN TAX SYSTEM

A study of the US fiscal system has been conducted from the perspective of competence between the federal government and the states, and more specifically the state of Nevada, as a primary step to the main objective of the investigation.

The US tax authority is the federal government, states, and local communities. This is what is called federalism and is enshrined both in the federal Constitution and the constitutions of the fifty states.[3]

Like the federal government, each state is governed by its own constitution. The state constitutions deal with the separation of powers and civil rights. They also contain provisions on the decentralization of authority between the central government of the state and the subdivisions of the state, including counties and municipalities.

It should be noted that this is a dual fiscal system,[4] in which the federal government and the states have their independence when it comes to regulating, managing, and executing their competences attributed in the Constitution of 1787.

---

3   Larry N. Gerston, *American Federalism: A Concise Introduction* (Armonk, NY: M.E. Sharpe, 2007), 91–139.
4   Gemma Martínez Bárbara, "Aproximación a los principios y fundamentos del modelo de federalismo fiscal de EE. UU. desde el Concierto Económico," in *Federalismo fiscal y concierto económico. Una aproximación desde el derecho comparado/ Federalismo fiskala eta kontzertu ekonomikoa. Zuzenbide konparatutik egindako hurbilketa* (Vitoria-Gasteiz: Eusko Legebiltzarra/Parlamento Vasco, 2016).

States can generally legislate on all matters within their territorial jurisdiction, including the fiscal one, with some restrictions that we will analyze later. This legislative power does not arise from the Constitution but is an inherent attribute of the sovereignty of the states. However, the Constitution provides certain limitations to that power.

Congress has various powers, such as financial authority, including the power to tax and spend to pay debts and provide for the common defense and general welfare of the United States. Congress also has the ability to borrow and appropriate money from the United States Treasury, and also has broad authority over the nation's commercial interests, the power to regulate commerce, provide bankruptcy laws, issue currency, establish post offices and highways, and grant patents and copyrights.

The Commerce Clause, which is discussed in more detail below, is one of the competencies of Congress.

Likewise, Congress has broad powers over public property, citizenship, and immigration as well as can regulating the time, place, and manner of federal elections and judging the outcome of such elections. Finally, Congress has numerous powers related to the protection of the United States and its sovereign interests.

In practice, there are matters in which there is competition between the federal government and states, and federal legislation generally prevails.

The dividing line between the competence of the state and the competence of the federal government is not always very clear, as is the case in matters of trade, which, if they affect international or interstate commerce is the responsibility of the federal government. In these cases, if the state decision does not have a substantial impact on the policy or the federal interest, it is very likely that a court will not declare that state decision unconstitutional.[5]

Likewise, there is a Supremacy Clause, in Article 6 of the Federal Constitution, which in case of conflict of powers, establishes that the federal law is supreme, and the courts, both federal and state, are obliged to recognize the supremacy of the federal law .

---

5   Walter Hellerstein, "The U.S. Supreme Court's State Tax Jurisprudence: A Template for Comparison," in *Comparative Fiscal Federalism: Comparing the European Court of Justice and the U.S. Supreme Court's Tax Jurisprudence*, ed. Reuven S. Avi-Yonah, James R. Hines Jr., and Michael Lang (Alphen aan den Rijn: Kluwer Law International; Frederick, MD: Sold and distributed in North, Central, and South America by Aspen Publishers, 2007).

The fiscal powers of the federal government are regulated in the Federal Tax Code (Internal Revenue Code, hereinafter IRC), whose application of the code is carried out by the jurisprudence of the Federal Tax Court (a tribunal with special jurisdiction over federal taxes) and the other federal courts of general jurisdiction, the federal courts of appeal, and the Supreme Court.

The Internal Revenue Service (IRS) is the federal agency of the government of the United States responsible for tax collection and compliance with tax laws. It is an agency within the Treasury Department of the United States and is also responsible for the interpretation and application of federal tax laws.

With respect to the tax revenue raising capacity, the federal government deposits most of the country's public income, as part of the federal revenues redistributed to the states, not in a uniform manner but mainly based on the economic data of the states and federal powers assumed by the states.

As mentioned above, the states have exclusive tax jurisdiction, except over import taxes, and it is worth highlighting the great difference in the tax system between each of them.

THE STATE OF NEVADA

The current Constitution of Nevada was adopted in 1864, and the government of the state of Nevada has a division of powers into executive, legislative, and judicial branches.

The principal official of the executive power of Nevada is the governor, elected by the population through state elections, for a term of up to four years.

The Nevada legislature is bicameral, that is, it is constituted by a senate and an assembly. Currently (2018), the senate is controlled by the Republican Party, and the assembly, by the Democratic Party.

The highest court in the judicial branch of Nevada is the Nevada Supreme Court, Nevada being one of the few American states without a system of intermediate appellate courts, and it is the Nevada Supreme Court that takes all cases and appeals. This court lacks discretionary review power, so the Nevada court system is highly congested.

Also, Nevada is one of the few states in which there is no personal income tax or corporate income tax in addition to federal taxes. The minimum statewide sales tax rate (burden with taxes the goods and services offered for retail sale, equivalent to value added tax or VAT, although with major differences) in Nevada is 6.5 percent. The municipalities have the power to also levy the sales tax, which makes the total sales tax rate in some areas rises to 8.25 percent.[6]

With reference to this sales tax, it should be noted that it is a tax that is only imposed by the states and municipalities, not by the federal government, and that differs fundamentally from the VAT in which the latter is charged in all operations, not only in the sale to final consumers and the goods and services are also liable to VAT, while goods and few services are only subject to the sale taxes (each state regulates the objective scope).

FISCAL LIMITATIONS OF THE STATES

The Constitution of 1787 makes no reference to the fiscal power of the states, although the legislators of the Constitution recognized the different fiscal interests of the states in the exercise of their fiscal powers and the nation's interest in promoting economic unity.

The Constitution contains two provisions (article 1.10 of the Constitution of the United States) restricting the general fiscal scope of state power.

In these provisions, it provides the tax authority of the federal government in imports and exports of goods and in law on tonnage.

There have been no substantive discussions on these two provisions of the import-export clause and the tonnage right because the first of these has been subsumed by the Commerce Clause and the second is only a specific area and in disuse.

So the most important topic and the limitation and origin of some problems of the taxation of the states is the Commerce Clause, which is explained in section 8 of article 1 of the Constitution and by which Congress will have power to regulate and enforce taxes to pay

---

6   State of Nevada, Office of the State Treasurer, *Annual Report - Fiscal Year 2017* (Las Vegas, 2018).

the debts and provide for the common defense and general welfare of the United States.

It also provides that the regulation of international and interstate commerce corresponds to the Congress and not to the states.

According to this power of the federal government backed by the jurisprudence of the Supreme Court, Congress has enacted relatively little legislation that affects the fiscal system of the states, although its legislative authority is unquestionable. Congress has the authority to regulate interstate commerce, to legislate state taxes in a uniform or harmonized manner for trade between states.

Moreover, the Supreme Court has expressly indicated that Congress has the power to legislate in a uniform manner the fiscal rules in relation to trade between the states. It has been observed in general that the Supreme Court has granted great flexibility to the states to legislate on fiscal matters, except for evident cases of certain fiscal benefits that harm the interstate commerce because they are discriminatory, which we will analyze later. Also, it has refused to intervene against fiscal competition between states to attract business, which is one of the most relevant characteristics in US fiscal policy, since Congress, with the so-called Dormant Commerce Clause for which it does not intervene in the fiscal regulation of interstate commerce, encourages the fiscal struggle between states.

A great difference can be observed with the EU tax system in which the states are sovereign in the fiscal area that also implies a financial autonomy of the same although with rules of harmonization, especially in the indirect taxes that we will analyze later.

It should be noted that most of the tax and social security collection in the US belongs to the federal government, and therefore the states do not have as much financial autonomy as the EU member countries do, as they depend on capital transfers of the federal government. In addition, another fundamental difference is that the US states do not have direct representation in Congress.

DIFFERENCES AND DISPUTES BETWEEN THE UNITED STATES AND THE EUROPEAN UNION

In the United States, federalism means that the federal government must respect the sovereignty of states with the limits established in the Constitution. Taxes are essential for sovereignty, and therefore, the Supreme Court has always maintained a permissive attitude to the fiscal regulation of the states in the matter of taxes, although it gives rise to a certain level of discrimination against other subjects that operate outside of that state. The Supreme Court only intervenes when the tax is absolutely discriminatory.

On the other hand, in the European Union there is no centralizing government. However, one of the objectives achieved by the European Union was to establish a single market, which must be perfected with fewer distortions through tax harmonization; this is one of the missions commissioned by the EU Commission, which advocates greater tax harmonization on direct taxes, understanding the absence of harmonization as a major obstacle to achieve this objective. In short, it is trying to achieve greater harmonization of direct taxes, such as the harmonization already used for indirect taxes. Thus, the VAT is harmonized in the European Union by the sixth Directive, adopted unanimously when the European Union had few member states and it was simply a unanimous agreement necessary for any change in tax harmonization.

The Supreme Court of the United States, in comparison with the European Union, is much more permissive in terms of state taxation in order to allow the states to compete for the location of the investment by the multinationals through the granting of tax incentives that has proved not to be very profitable for the states, and even less for the overall benefit of the United States, creating a harmful tax competition called "race to the bottom," in which the states only grant incentives to prevent multinationals from going to other states, not because they believe that the benefits of investment really justify the opportunity cost in lost tax revenues. In Europe, such incentives are prohibited by so-called state aid under the Treaty of the European Union, which does not allow aid to certain companies.

This is one of the essential differences with the European system, in which lately one can see certain decisions imposed by the European Commission on American technology companies, as was the case of

Apple in 2016 and Starbucks in 2017. Other companies are presently being studied in this regard, including Google, Amazon, and others like Fiat, with European roots.

Regarding the Apple issue, the European Commission decreed that the government of Ireland should demand from Apple more than 13,000 million euros plus interest on delay, for having signed an illegal "tax ruling," according to the European Treaty and considered a state aid to the Apple company for granting it illegal tax benefits, which has allowed Apple to pay far less taxes than other companies in Ireland.

Specifically, a tax rate of corporate income tax was applied for more than ten years that was much lower than the general rate for companies, the first year at 1 percent and decreasing thereafter until, in the last year of verification, 2014, the effective rate was 0.005 percent, while Ireland's tax rate was 12.5 percent, approximately half of the European average rate on corporate income tax.[7]

In fact, thanks to the tax ruling that was applied in Ireland, Apple was able to avoid the imposition of almost all the profits generated by the sales of its products in the single market of the European Union as a whole. This is due to the decision of this company to register all its sales in Ireland instead of in the countries where the products in question were sold.

In principle, the rules on EU state aid require the recovery of incompatible state aid in order to eliminate the distortion of competition caused by them. The EU state aid rules do not impose sanctions, and the recovery does not penalize the company in question but simply restores equal treatment in relation to the other companies.

This decision on the application of state aid has been appealed by Apple and the Irish government.

Likewise, it is worth mentioning the official opposition of the United States to such a decision of the European Commission, through the report issued by the Treasury Department of the United States, which considers that this decision has great implications for the United States, both for the government and for US companies:

- The United States has made many efforts to develop the BEPS report together with the other G20 countries.

---

7   http://europa.eu/rapid/press-release_IP-16-2923_en.htm.

- There is a possibility that it is a transfer of public income from American families and from the federal government to the Inland Revenue of European countries.

- There are a substantial number of American companies affected by the same measures, and it is possible they are being persecuted.

- For technical purposes, considering that the decision is against the law, it is a retroactive application that puts at risk the legal security of certain companies.

As one can see there is a clear disparity in what is considered aid between the European Union and the United States, since the latter does not contemplate aid, unless it may violate the principle of discrimination in the Commerce Clause.

There is also a serious problem for US companies and possible taxation in the United States for partaking of the benefits corresponding to the parent company or headquarters in which research work is carried out, among other functions.

INTERNATIONAL TAXATION MEASURES

In line with these disputes and as the United States argued in the aforementioned official document against the decision of the European Commission in the Apple case, a tool has been developed in recent years to prevent the transfer of benefits from countries in which there is real multinational activity in countries with low or no taxation through the BEPS report promoted by the OECD and signed by more than one hundred countries, including the G20 countries.

These measures were taken by the OECD because the international tax scenario is constantly changing due to the substantial economic change resulting from growing globalization, necessitating the change of new fiscal rules to protect the public revenues of the countries. The BEPS Report[8] aims to avoid fiscal strategies that artificially seek to divert the profits of multinationals to territories of low taxation in which they do not conduct economic activity or only conduct activity of little importance.

---

8   http://www.oecd.org/tax/beps/.

One of the fifteen measures of the BEPS Report is the application of transfer pricing between related entities in order to avoid the transfer of benefits pertaining to the country in which the main activity is carried out through corporate networks to other countries of low taxation in which they are established yet inactive.

It is worth noting the great similarities between the current transfer pricing policies between US and European regulations due to the adoption of the BEPS project report. However, there have been differences in the transfer pricing previously, since the OECD guidelines were not applied and American regulation has been in continuous evolution and established as an internal law.

Therefore, we can say that in transfer pricing there are no substantial differences due to the application of the OECD guidelines.

Another of the measures proposed by the OECD to prevent the tax fraud is the automatic exchange of information (AEOI) through the CRS (Common Reporting and Due Diligence) system by which the tax administrations of the member countries are allowed to periodically have tax information on the investments or positions of its taxpayers in financial institutions located abroad.

This system proposed by the OECD has been signed by more than one hundred countries, including all member states of the European Union, China, India, Russia, low-taxation territories such as the Isle of Man, the Cayman Islands, Singapore, and others. Incomprehensibly, the CRS has yet to be signed by United States, although it is required, through the FATCA Law (the Law on Compliance Foreign Accounts Tax), to share fiscal information with other countries.

The origin of the CRS was the FATCA approved by the US Congress in 2010 and in force since 2013, which the United States enacted to improve tax compliance for US taxpayers. Some US taxpayers had been evading US income tax.

The purpose of the FATCA provision is to control tax evasion against the federal government by identifying the citizens and residents of that country who have money or funds deposited in foreign financial entities. In order to do this, all financial entities outside of the United States (known as FFIs) are required to identify and report to US citizens and residents who have deposits and investments in those banks. They must make available to the IRS information related to accounts and other financial products of said persons.

FATCA wants FFIs to register with the American tax agency (the Internal Revenue or IRS) and declare the financial results of their US clients or pay a 30 percent withholding on all their financial income from US sources. Several countries, including Spain, have signed international agreements (AIG) with the United States, by virtue of which FFIs can present declarations required according to the FATCA in the tax authority.

In other words and although it is unusual, the United States sometimes does require financial information from other countries and, on the other hand, does not want to provide financial data of foreign taxpayers who have their accounts in their country.

In line with this information, it should be noted that there are states such as Nevada and Wyoming that do not have the obligation to declare the owners of the bank accounts to the authorities; this is called bank secrecy, and it has previously been implemented by Switzerland. Therefore, many foreign investors are taking their great fortunes to these states instead of to other jurisdictions such as the British Virgin Islands, the Cayman Islands, or Switzerland because they may no longer be able to continue with bank secrecy, mainly due to the AEOI.

On the other hand, the United States has signed the country-by-country agreement for the exchange of tax information.

THE COMMERCE CLAUSE

As stated above, the regulation of international and interstate commerce corresponds to Congress and not to the states.

Also, the so-called Dormant Commerce Clause[9] is a power not used by the federal government since Congress has not enacted legislation that affects the fiscal system of the states, although its legislative authority is unquestionable. Congress has the authority to regulate interstate commerce and to legislate on state taxes in a uniform or harmonized manner for trade between states.

Ultimately, the Supreme Court has delimited the Dormant Commerce Clause in order to allow states to fiscally incentivize companies to promote economic development within their borders.

---

9   Brent B. Nicholson and Sue Mota, "The Dormant Commerce Clause Rises Again: Cuno v. Daimler Chrysler," *Houston Business and Tax Law Journal* 5 (2005), 322–40.

Relevant cases of the Supreme Court's Case Law:[10]
Boston Stock Market (1977)

In this case, the Supreme Court considered that the tax incentive on the tax on the transfer of shares violated the commercial clause and was therefore null.

First, this case concerned a New York Stock Transfer Tax that applied to all stock transfers, regardless of where the sale of shares occurred. However, in order to attract nonresident stock sellers to make their sales through brokerage in New York, rather than in any other state, the state of New York modified the regulations to offer these sellers a tax incentive similar to the residents in New York.

Therefore, the tax incentive was the same for residents or nonresidents as long as the sale was made through the mediators of New York. Faced with this situation, the Court found that this tax incentive was contrary to the principle of the Commerce Clause, since it would be discriminatory with respect to other states and a seller would be induced to trade through a New York broker to reduce its tax burden in the transfer of securities, thus providing a tax incentive for sellers to deal with New York instead of out-of-state brokers.

The judgment explains that states are not prevented from structuring their fiscal systems to promote the growth and development of intrastate commerce through the use of fiscal incentives, provided they are not contrary to the Commerce Clause. However, it does not explain how it can achieve the objective to encourage the growth and competitiveness of companies without affecting said clause and without being discriminatory between resident sellers of the state and nonresidents.

Bacchus (1984)

In the judgment of Bacchus Imports, Ltd., a tax exemption on alcohol was considered contrary to the Commerce Clause because it was directed only to alcoholic beverages produced locally.

---

10   Walter Hellerstein and Dan T. Coenen, "Commerce Clause Restraints on State Business Development Incentives," *Cornell Law Review* 81, no. 4 (May 1996), 789–878.

That is, the state applied a tax benefit to the products in which certain alcohol produced in a certain state was used, and according to the Court, this discriminatory exemption is considered against products manufactured outside that state, and therefore this violates Commerce Clause, which prohibits said exemption.

However, this sentence recalls the possibility of states, through tax incentives, helping their local economy without harming other businessmen from other states.

WESTINGHOUSE (1984)

In this case, the judgment declared contrary to the Commerce Clause an aid "Franchise taxes" (taxes imposed on conducting business in the states) for sales made from New York to other states.

The court understood that in addition to encouraging New York companies, it did not allow other companies resident in other states to compete, which would be discriminatory for interstate commerce and therefore violated the Dormant Clause Commerce, since this tax incentive promoted the business of one state, given the tax burden on the same business performed outside of this much larger state.

D. ARMCO (1984)

In this case, the Supreme Court ruled that there was discrimination between residents and nonresidents of a state that violated the Interstate Commerce Clause, since the state of West Virginia taxed in the individual income tax the sale of tangible materials but allowed the exemption for producers residing in that state.

Armco denounced this assumption as it understood that the Interstate Commerce Clause is not complied with, and this argument was accepted by the Supreme Court, even though the state of West Virginia considered that there is no discrimination, since other states, specifically the state where Armco resides, is subject to the manufacturing tax to a lesser extent compared to West Virginia, and that it is a compensation for that difference.

The Supreme Court of the United States rejected these allegations of the state of West Virginia and the Supreme Court of that state, indicating that they are different taxes and that West Virginia also has the possibility of imposing a higher manufacturing tax, considering this tax incentive to be discriminatory residents in West Virginia.

NEW ENERGY (1988)

In this case, the Supreme Court also found contrary to the Commercial Clause a tax incentive granted by the state of Ohio and consisting of a tax credit on the production of a fuel called Gasohol, providing the Ethanol produced in the state of Ohio.

The Court considered this tax incentive to be discriminatory since it harmed other products not subject to said tax incentive. The state of Ohio considered that using other aid, such as a state subsidy that favors such companies, could have obtained the same result; this claim was dismissed by the Court, which argued that said tax credit was contrary to the Interstate Commerce Clause.

Here you can see a difference with respect to the European Union in which state aid is not allowed, as in the United States if it violates the Interstate Commerce Clause, but direct aid through a subsidy would be legal.

CAMPS NEWFOUND / OWATONNA (1997)

Also, as in the other judgments described above, the Supreme Court declared the exemption in the real estate tax discriminatory because it violated the Commerce Clause since it applied to entities with charitable purposes if the main beneficiaries of these institutions were resident persons in the state of Maine.

The present judgment was approved by five to four judges, having dismissed the claim by the Supreme Court of the state of Maine.

Cuno v. Daimler Chrysler (2006)

The Supreme Court of the United States annulled the tax credit in the corporate franchise tax (state tax levied on certain companies) that the state of Ohio had granted to the Daimler Company for the construction of a large factory as long as said investment was made in Ohio.

On the contrary, the Court considered the exemption in the property tax for several years to be legal, since it was not discriminatory and did not violate the Free Trade Clause.

Yet it did in the tax credit since it considered, like the eighteen complainants, that this tax incentive discriminated against the activity of interstate commerce, since it benefited the companies that invested in this state and not those companies that made the same investment outside of said state, forcing them to invest in a certain state.

This difference of opinion between the exemption in the real estate tax and the tax credit in the Corporate Franchise Tax is explained in said judgment, arguing by the Court that no business is discriminated in the exemption to be made in one state or in another.

Conclusions

It is worth highlighting the Cuno decision because of its importance, since many states applied those tax credits that were declared contrary to the Commercial Clause and, on the other hand, the exemptions in the real estate tax were perfectly allowed as well. Next, we will talk about the subsidies of the states to companies that are not contracted to this clause since they are not fiscal incentives.

Of all these cases, the following conclusion can be drawn:

In order to be considered contrary to the Commerce Clause, the following requirements must be met:

-First, that the state favors business activity within the state outside the state.

- Second, that the state grants fiscal benefits in favor of said activities.

NEXUS

Nexus can be defined[11] as the relationship or connection in the scope of taxation between a state and a taxpayer in order to determine to what state and in what proportion the tax levy corresponds. Thus, it is a necessary and often controversial element due to the tax differences between the different states.

Until 1992 the Supreme Court of the United States had considered that the nexus, without differentiation between taxes, depended basically on the physical presence of the taxpayer in the state, regardless of where sales were made, intangible assets, or other elements.

However, starting in 1992, with the *Quill Corp. v. North Carolina* case, the Supreme Court differentiated between the nexus that must exist between taxes, demanding in the case of indirect taxes that there be a physical presence; however, this was not necessary for the other taxes.

In recent years and due to the increasing valuation of intangible assets, many states have changed the nexus required for their taxation in proportion to three factors: property, employment, and sales.

It is worth noting the change of taxation in the states in which there was no physical presence, as in the case of Amazon, which faced the various criticisms decided in 2017 to change its fiscal strategy, going on to pay taxes in all the states that have sales taxes   independently that does not have a physical presence and taxes at the destination depending on the recipient of the operation.

This question generates a lot of debate because, as in the case of Amazon, many sales made over the Internet remain or were not taxed because it was not considered that enough of a nexus existed.

NEXUS IN THE ECONOMIC AGREEMENT

The Economic Agreement distributes competence between the Basque Country and the Spanish state, in relation to legislative, tax inspection, and levying powers concerning each of the agreed tax figures within the tax systems of the Historical Territories.

---

11   Walter Hellerstein, "A Primer on State Tax Nexus: Law, Power, and Policy," *55 St. Tax Notes* 555, February 22, 2010.

The tax nexus are the allocating criteria to determine who pays taxes in the Basque Country, in what proportion, and according to which tax law (state or *foral*).

Therefore, they are distribution models that differ mainly in that the American distribution model has no regulation that establishes the allocating criteria but is created by the jurisprudence of the Supreme Court. On the other hand, the Basque Country has established criteria through the Economic Agreement.

In addition, in the Economic Agreement, unlike in the American tax system, there is an Arbitration Board[12] for the resolution of tax disputes between the administrations before going to the Supreme Court.

CORPORATE INCOME TAX AND ITS HARMONIZATION IN THE UNITED STATES AND EUROPEAN UNION

First, in the United States there are nine main forms of business organizations, which are regulated and taxed by each state independently.[13] The most important are LLC, Corporation C, S Corporation, and Association. Corporation C is the only one that is directly taxed to the business organization, which is taxed as a company according to the corporate income tax in the European Union.

There are two administrations that impose the corporate income tax, the federal government and the states.

Most states have developed solid tax systems designed to tax business income. Each state has designed its own corporation tax, although all of them have important similarities, since no state has ventured to reinvent the federal corporation tax, regulated in the Internal Revenue Code (IRC). Generally, the state corporation tax takes as a starting point the federal tax base and the accounting principles and concepts of the federal regulation are the foundation of the tax regulations of various states.

---

12 Committee in charge of solving conflicts that arise between the Basque Country and the state administration or between the Basque Country and the autonomous communities, in relation to the application of the Economic Agreement to particular tax relations and to other matters concerning the distribution of competences.
13 David J. Cartano, *Federal and State Taxation of Limited Liability Companies* (Chicago: Wolters Kluwer, 2017).

Companies that conduct their commercial and economic activity in more than one state pose some problems of tax distribution. Thus, a company can manufacture a product in the state of Nevada, store it in California, and sell it through a sales office in Texas, for the consumption of customers residing in Florida. These four states have the capacity to tax a part of the income generated, only limited by federal legislation. The complicated aspect is to determine what part of said income can be taxed by each state. The need to divide the tax base between the different jurisdictions involved does not only affect the states, but any jurisdiction that intends to exercise its tax power.

These difficulties are related to the problem of the Economic Agreement in the tax allocating criteria, which are solved by the Arbitration Board, or in case of appeal, as in the ROVER case (for the VAT allocating criterion of intra-community transactions) by the Supreme Court, although recently (February 2016) two judgments have been issued by the Supreme Court indicating a change of criteria.

In the case of states, it is only the judiciary that is responsible for this (state courts and, in cases of discrepancy in business interests, the US Supreme Court).

Continuing with the issue of corporate tax of the states, American companies are taxed based on their worldwide income, as in the Basque internal regulations, and since there is also the possibility of taxing the same income in more than one jurisdiction, these companies can benefit from a tax credit for taxes paid in other jurisdictions by reducing the amount of corporation tax payable to the federal government and the states. Generally, foreign companies are taxed in the United States (with some exceptions) based on the income generated within their borders.

In general, corporate tax can be implemented in two different ways: a) through the so-called franchise tax, which involves imposing a tax on companies for the privilege of carrying out their economic activity within the state in question, measured on the basis of income, b) through the direct taxation of the benefits derived, or that may be attributed, to the state of taxation.

The US Constitution allows states to assess a part of the income of companies, as long as there is a sufficient connection or relationship with that state (nexus). The existence of a link implies that the income that is subject to taxation derives from the activities carried out by the company within the borders of the state that imposes the tax. Therefore, a state (other than the constitution of the company) may impose a part, or all, of the income of a company, as long as they are effectively the product of the operations and commercial activities of that company in this state. For this, at the state level there are three procedures to determine the income of companies that may be subject to taxation, according to the parameters established by the Constitution of the United States: 1) separate accounting, 2) the formula of apportionment, and 3) the specific imputation.

The system of the apportionment formula is the most widespread and currently used. The separate accounting, in its day commonly used, has lost its validity today. Consequently, the number of litigations is increasingly abundant, since companies that operate in more than one state consider that there is sometimes double taxation on the same income with the corresponding loss of competitiveness that this entails. On the other hand, those companies whose operations are intrastate (their economic activity takes place only in one state) argue that large companies, whose businesses take place interstate, have a greater capacity to create much more sophisticated tax structures than those that are its scope, in order to minimize the fiscal impact.

Once the problem is summarized when establishing the tax base for the American corporate income tax of companies operating in different states, it is considered necessary to study the principle of collaboration between the states, or in their case, the decision-making bodies of possible conflicts.

This same problem exists in Europe and that is the reason for the development of the BEPS project, which follows the same principle of full competition in the United States and Europe.

FEDERAL CORPORATION TAX[14]

The federal corporation tax in the United States had the highest marginal tax rates (35 percent) in the world (before the Trump Tax reform), and companies had responded by changing their businesses, their income, and their residences abroad in some cases. Meanwhile, the companies

---

14 Ephraim P. Smith, Philip J. Harmelink, and James R. Hasselback, *CCH Federal Taxation Basic Principles* (Chicago: Wolters Kluwer, 2015).

that do not pay for the corporate income tax (CIT) pay taxes on natural persons and face very high rates as well.

At the international level, the tax rate is even higher in comparison with the more developed countries in recent years, as the average rate of the CIT at the international level has decreased considerably, while it has remained the same in the United States.

However, there are certain legal figures, such as the Trust, that greatly reduce the tax burden and are driven by certain states that favor the attraction of capital.

In addition, the US corporate tax system discouraged investment, a central driver of economic growth, and has been modified the tax radically with Trump's legislative reform, which advocates a lower tax burden and proposed to lower the tax rate in its tax reform from 35 percent to 21 percent the (CIT).

STATE CORPORATION INCOME TAX

This tax is collected in forty-four states. Although it is often thought to be a large collection tax, it represents only 5.4 percent of state revenues and 2.7 percent of general revenues.

The state of Iowa imposes the highest corporate state tax rate, at 12 percent. Iowa is closely followed by Pennsylvania (9.99 percent) and Minnesota (9.8 percent). Three other states (Alaska, Connecticut, and New Jersey) and the District of Columbia have tax rates of 9 percent or more.

By contrast, the North Carolina fixed rate of 3 percent is the lowest rate in the country, followed by rates in North Dakota (4.31 percent) and Colorado (4.63 percent). Four other states impose rates below 5 percent: Arizona at 4.9 percent and Mississippi, South Carolina, and Utah at 5 percent.

Since South Dakota and Wyoming do not impose corporate tax or other direct taxes on companies, other states such as Nevada, Ohio, Texas, Washington, Delaware, and Virginia do not impose CIT either.

DIFFERENCES IN TAX HARMONIZATION IN CORPORATE INCOME TAX BETWEEN THE UNITED STATES AND THE EUROPEAN UNION

It is worth mentioning the international changes in taxation due to the existing fraud of large companies that take advantage of the weaknesses of the international tax system, which allows them to divert the benefits subject to taxation to countries with low or no taxation or to take advantage of the agreements of double taxation that allow full tax exemption due to the nonexistence of multilateral agreements between different countries.

Given this situation, important international initiatives have been carried out, mainly proposed by the OECD, the G20, and within the European Union through the Commission and other organizations.

It is worth highlighting with respect to the tax on companies in the European Union the proposal of the 2001 BICCIS Directive that proposes the harmonization of the Tax Base for Corporate Income Taxes at Community level (not at the level of tax rates), which was not approved by the Council and was restated through two directives published on October 25, 2016, a Directive establishing a Common Corporate Tax Base (BICIS) and a Directive establishing a Common Consolidated Tax Base (CCCTB).

On March 13, 2018, the Council reached agreement on a proposal aimed at boosting transparency in order to tackle aggressive cross-border tax planning. It will require intermediaries such as tax advisors, accountants, and lawyers that design or promote tax planning schemes to report schemes that are considered potentially aggressive, and it will apply as of July 1, 2020.[15]

The purpose of these directives is, on the one hand, the reduction of administrative costs for companies, since currently EU companies have to meet the requirements of twenty-eight different taxation systems of companies, which can pose a considerable administrative burden considerable and an obstacle to cross-border investment in the European Union.

On the other hand, the purpose is also to help the member states to fight against aggressive tax planning—because in the current international

---

15   http://www.consilium.europa.eu/en/press/press-releases/2018/03/13/corporate-tax-avoidance-agreement-reached-on-tax-intermediaries/.

economic environment, with increasingly globalized, mobile, and digital business models and with the complex structures of multinational companies, it is difficult for governments to ensure that the income of companies is taxed in the countries where the value is created. There are large differences between the corporate tax regimes from one EU member state to another, and these differences create favorable conditions for transnational corporations to establish tax planning systems, which generally consist of transferring their benefits to low tax jurisdictions.

In addition to these last measures for harmonization in corporate income tax, the Ministers of Finance of the European Union have found that large companies pay taxes depending on the country in which they provide their services at the destination. However, the problem for the agreement is that countries with low taxation in Europe do not agree, and unanimity is required from the current twenty-eight member countries.

The tax harmonization of the corporation income tax in the United States does not exist since there is no legislative initiative on the part of the federal government, which would have such a power, nor does the so-called "soft law" of the European Union exist, nor does consensus exist among the different states to implement a policy that tends towards the tax harmonization between federal and the different states.[16]

Similarly, in the European Union the objectives of the member countries are different and there is also competition among them to attract of large companies through tax incentives.

However, in the European Union there is greater harmonization, coordination, and, above all, collaboration among member states than exists in the United States among the states at the official level.

The main differences between the United States and the European Union in the harmonization of the corporate income tax are the following:

1. Tax nexus to establish the location of the income. It has already been mentioned previously that there is no unanimity in the applied criteria and it is object of controversy between the different states, except agreements between different states, which I will explain later.

---

16 Charles E. McLure, Jr., "Harmonizing Corporate Income Taxes in the US and the EU: Legislative, Judicial, Soft Law and Cooperative Approaches," *Cesifo Forum* 2 (2008), 46–52.

2. Lack of coordination and harmonization between the federal government and the states because the federal government, despite having the power granted by the Constitution on the regulation of interstate commerce, has not acted in favor of greater coordination and harmonization. On the other hand, in the European Union, the Commission acts as the driving force behind harmonization measures of the European Union, which is the official body that looks after the interests of the European Union as a whole and making important proposals such as the Directive establishing a Common Corporate Tax Base (BICIS) and the Directive establishing a Common Consolidated Tax Base (CCCTB).

3. The Constitution of the United States does not contain specifically in its legislation, as in the Treaty of the European Union, articles on the freedom of movement of persons, property, capital, and establishment. However, the jurisprudence of the Supreme Court leads to the same interpretation criteria as in Europe.

4. The so-called soft law of the European Union does not exist in the United States, which generates less coordination and collaboration.

5. The scarce harmonization, collaboration, and coordination between the states is done through agreements between them or mediated by various associations that I will quote below. However, it should be noted that there exist several American associations that promote collaboration and coordination between the states, which I will mention below.

Multistate Tax Commission (MTC)

The MTC is an intergovernmental state tax agency that was founded in 1967, with the objectives of promoting equity and coherence in the fiscal policy of the states and preserving fiscal sovereignty in both states and municipalities.

To achieve these objectives, it raises tax uniformity and equity at the level of the states without taking into account the harmonization with the federal government.

Twenty-three member states that follow their proposals and twenty-six participate as collaborators in the work carried out by the commission.

The programs they use to achieve the goal of harmonization are mainly:

Nexus: This is a program that determines in which state the tax should be taxed in the most just, effective way, and without double taxation. Currently, thirty-eight states collaborate in this program.

Joint Audit Program: This is a program of coordination of tax inspections among the collaborating states in order to coordinate the verification actions in direct and indirect taxes.

FEDERATION OF TAX ADMINISTRATORS (FTA)

The FTA is a nonprofit association created in 1937 for the purpose of coordination and collaboration among the different tax administrations of the country, to achieve a more effective tax system.

Collaborating members of this association are the different tax agencies of the states, such as the IRS, and the tools to meet this objective are the exchange of information and coordination between administrations and the investigation and avoidance of tax fraud.

It is worth mentioning the differences between these two fiscal entities: although their common objective is to improve the efficiency of the American fiscal system, MTC aims to harmonize fiscal systems between the states without federal government participation, while FTA coordinates and collaborates among all US tax administrations, including, obviously, the IRS.

In short, there are, in addition to MTC and FTA, other entities that in some way support and promote tax harmonization, collaboration, and coordination in the United States but without the clear impetus of the IRS, although these functions are granted by the Constitution to the federal government through the IRS.

SALES TAX AND DIFFERENCES WITH VALUE ADDED TAX (VAT)

Sales tax is a tax of indirect nature applied to goods and in some states services and that is only supported by the final consumer.

It differs from VAT mainly in that only the last phase is taxed, that is to say, the final consumer and not in all phases, as in VAT (its operation is simpler than VAT), and it does not fall on most services and intangible assets.

Also, it should be noted that it is a tax currently levied by forty-five states, ranging from up to 10 percent in Louisiana and Tennessee to no taxing at all in five states: Alaska, Delaware, Montana, New Hampshire, and Oregon.

It is worth noting that in the same state there are differences in sales tax, which means that certain municipalities have competitive advantages over others and that they are not considered illegal. What causes this system of indirect taxation is a tax competition between the different states and municipalities because of the differences in rates, and in some cases purchases are made online without sales tax for the purpose of tax avoidance.

A big problem that has existed in the collection of sales tax is that online sales were not taxed because the federal regulations determine that there must be a physical link, which is the physical presence of the selling company in the state that taxes the sale.[17]

For many years the majority of online sales have not been taxed despite the growing volume of sales by this method, and the consequences are twofold: first, the unfair economic advantage of online sellers, and second, the loss of revenue of the states and municipalities.

This "loophole" is due to the fact that it is a tax not regulated by the federal government (unlike the VAT in the European Union) as well as the lack of harmonization and fiscal coordination between the different tax jurisdictions in the United States.

However, progress has been made between the states to tax online operations under the sales tax, although Congress has not yet implemented its harmonizing capacity provided for in the Constitution.

---

17 Walter Hellerstein, "Taxing Remote Sales in the Digital Age: A Global Perspective," 65 *American Law University Review* (2016), 1195–1239.

As a relevant example of these advances, in 2017 Amazon began collecting sales tax for all its sales from final consumers of all the states, before any great pressure was exerted by business leaders and political parties.

BASQUE COUNTRY TAX HARMONIZATION WITHIN THE CURRENT INTERNATIONAL SCENARIO

How does fiscal harmonization as well as the new change of international scenario affect the tax competences of Basque Country administrations?

First, it should be noted, as established in article 2, fifth paragraph of the Economic Agreement, that the Basque Tax System should be subject to "Submission to the International Agreements or Treaties signed and ratified or adhered to by the Spanish state. In particular, it shall comply with the provisions laid down in the International Agreements signed by Spain to avoid double taxation, as well as fiscal harmonization measures of the European Union, and shall be responsible for making the refunds called for, pursuant to application of said Agreements and rules."

Therefore, it must incorporate the international fiscal measures agreed by Spain with the other countries, such as the OECD measures such as BEPS report, or the directive of the European Union published on July 12, 2016, a directive laying down rules against tax avoidance practices that directly affect the functioning of the internal market.

On the other hand,[18] it is worth mentioning that the Basque Country did not participate in international forums such as the OECD or the European Union until 2011, when, after years of political struggle, the Spanish government agreed that representatives of the Basque Country (currently through the Biscay Tax Administration) could participate directly, integrating the delegation of the Spanish state into some working groups of ECOFIN.

---

18 Gemma Martínez Bárbara, "Tax Harmonization in Federal Systems: The Basque Case," in *The Basque Fiscal System Contrasted to Nevada and Catalonia in the Time of Major Crises*, ed. Joseba Agirreazkuenaga and Xabier Irujo (Reno: Center for Basque Studies, University of Nevada, Reno, 2016).

CONCLUSION

On the one hand, with regard to internal fiscal harmonization, collaboration, and coordination within the European Union and the United States, there are important differences between them. The European Union has a greater level of fiscal harmonization than does the United States due to the harmonizing work of the European Commission (the so-called guardian of the Treaty), which is supported by the European Court of Justice (ECJ). Notable differences include the harmonization of indirect taxes, the consideration of state aid, the so-called soft law, with proposals such as the Common Consolidated Corporate Tax Base that aims to address among other things of double taxation, non-taxation, calculation of transfer pricing, and reduction of high costs for taxpayers in operations among member states.

However, this tax harmonization function conducted by the European Commission has not been undertaken by the US Congress, through the IRS, which is not "the guardian of the Constitution," even though it is legitimized by the US Constitution, and this fiscal harmonization inactivity is supported by the Supreme Court, which defends the fiscal sovereignty of the states in tax matters, except certain cases that are clearly discriminatory.

One of the reasons for these harmonizing differences between the European Union and the United States is legal-political,[19] due to member states of the EU having different historical backgrounds and different legal regulations. From my point of view, there is also another reason that should not be ignored: the different economic approaches in the United States and the European Union, because the United States prioritizes tax competition over fiscal coordination and harmonization due to the theoretical economic advantages.

Regarding to the possible comparison at the level of the state of Nevada and Basque Country, as I explained above there are some important differences between the legal powers of each one of them. The Basque Country is a fiscal harmonized jurisdiction at the level of Spain and the European Union, and one of the most important differences between Nevada and the Basque Country is the latter's fiscal

---

19 Reuven S. Avi-Yonah, "What Can the U.S. Supreme Court and the European Court of Justice Learn from Each Other's Tax Jurisprudence?" *Michigan International Lawyer* 18, no. 3 (2006), 1–3.

and financial autonomy, which arises from the Economic Agreement between the Basque Country and Spain, the former being (with Navarre) the federal region with the greatest fiscal and financial autonomy at the international level.

On the other hand, in the last five years at the level of international taxation, both in the European Union and the United States, great changes have been made, with greater collaboration among countries in the exchange of fiscal and financial information, and with measures such as the BEPS project, AEOI, Country by Country Reporting, and Multilateral Tax Agreements, among others, which advocate a change in the international tax picture, including much more information for the fiscal authorities and therefore unheard of transparency.

BIBLIOGRAPHY

Avi-Yonah, Reuven S. "What Can the U.S. Supreme Court and the European Court of Justice Learn from Each Other's Tax Jurisprudence?" *Michigan International Lawyer* 18, no. 3 (2006): 1–3.

Cartano, David J. *Federal and State Taxation of Limited Liability Companies*. Chicago: Wolters Kluwer, 2017.

Gerston, Larry N. *American Federalism: A Concise Introduction*. Armonk, NY: M.E. Sharpe, 2007.

Hellerstein, Walter. "The U.S. Supreme Court's State Tax Jurisprudence: A Template for Comparison." In *Comparative Fiscal Federalism: Comparing the European Court of Justice and the U.S. Supreme Court's Tax Jurisprudence*, edited by Reuven S. Avi-Yonah, James R. Hines Jr., and Michael Lang. Alphen aan den Rijn: Kluwer Law International; Frederick, MD: Sold and distributed in North, Central, and South America by Aspen Publishers, 2007.

———. "A Primer on State Tax Nexus: Law, Power, and Policy." *55 St. Tax Notes* 555, February 22, 2010.

———. "Taxing Remote Sales in the Digital Age: A Global Perspective." *65 American Law University Review* (2016): 1195–1239.

Hellerstein, Walter, and Dan T. Coenen. "Commerce Clause Restraints on State Business Development Incentives." *Cornell Law Review* 81, no. 4 (May 1996): 789–878.

Martínez Bárbara, Gemma. "Aproximación a los principios y fundamentos del modelo de federalismo fiscal de EE. UU. desde el Concierto Económico." In *Federalismo fiscal y concierto económico. Una aproximación desde el derecho comparado/Federalismo fiskala eta kontzertu ekonomikoa. Zuzenbide konparatutik egindako hurbilketa.* Vitoria-Gasteiz: Eusko Legebiltzarra/Parlamento Vasco, 2016.

———. "Tax Harmonization in Federal Systems: The Basque Case." In *The Basque Fiscal System Contrasted to Nevada and Catalonia in the Time of Major Crises*, edited by Joseba Agirreazkuenaga and Xabier Irujo. Reno: Center for Basque Studies, University of Nevada, Reno, 2016.

McLure, Jr., Charles E. "Harmonizing Corporate Income Taxes in the US and the EU: Legislative, Judicial, Soft Law and Cooperative Approaches." *Cesifo Forum* 2 (2008): 46–52.

Nicholson, Brent B., and Sue Mota. "The Dormant Commerce Clause Rises Again: Cuno v. Daimler Chrysler." *Houston Business and Tax Law Journal* 5 (2005): 322–40.

Smith, Ephraim P., Philip J. Harmelink, and James R. Hasselback. *CCH Federal Taxation Basic Principles*. Chicago: Wolters Kluwer, 2015.

State of Nevada, Office of the State Treasurer. *Annual Report - Fiscal Year 2017*. Las Vegas, 2018.

Chapter 4

A Comparison between Wealth Transfer Taxes in the Basque Autonomous Community and the United States

Aitziber Etxebarria Usategi

John Locke said: "The reason why men enter into society, is the preservation of their property."[1] At present, property rights continue to rule our economy and wealth transfers go hand in hand with private property. The purpose of this chapter is to explain and compare wealth transfer taxes in the Basque Autonomous Community and in the United States. In order to do so, the chapter starts with a brief review of the historical background of the law systems these territories are based on. American taxes will then be described and compared to Basque ones, with special attention to the relationships among states and the federal government as well as between the Basque Autonomous Community and the Spanish government and the European Union, through the Basque Economic Agreement. At the end of this chapter, different opinions about the future of both tax systems will be presented.

American and Basque Legal Traditions and Inheritance Laws

Nowadays, there are two major legal traditions in the world: common law and civil law or Roman law. The common law tradition appeared in

---

1   John Locke, "Of the Dissolution of Government," in *Second Treatise of Civil Government* (1690).

England during the Middle Ages and was subsequently implemented in the British colonies across different continents. The civil law tradition was developed in continental Europe at the same time and was later applied in the colonies of other European imperial powers. In the nineteenth and twentieth centuries, the civil law tradition was also adopted by countries with different legal traditions, such as Russia and Japan, in order to achieve economic and political power comparable to that of Western European countries. Thus, the legal tradition of the Basque Autonomous Community is based on civil law, whereas common law is the basis of the legal traditions of the United States, except for Louisiana, which has a hybrid system of both traditions.

Common law is mostly uncodified since there is no comprehensive compilation of legal rules and statutes. It is mostly based on precedents in similar cases. Consequently, judges have a remarkable role in shaping law. Common law functions as an adversarial system in which a dispute between two opposite parties goes before a judge who moderates the case.

Civil law systems have complete legal codes that are continuously updated. These legal codes stipulate all issues, including those prosecuted before a court, the valid procedure, and the appropriate punishment for each offense. The judge establishes the facts of the case and applies the provisions of the pertinent code.[2]

As far as the inheritance tradition is concerned, during the colonial period the United States adopted English inheritance law, which is ruled by the principle of testamentary freedom. After independence, most states enacted statutes based on English common law with some modifications. During westward expansion, some new states adopted aspects of civil law like community-property (Arizona, California, Idaho, Nevada, New Mexico, Texas, Washington, Wisconsin, and Alaska).[3] In a community property state, each spouse owns a one-half interest in the marital property bought with work income during the marriage. The rest of the states are ruled by common law. In a common law state, ownership is settled by the name on the title or by verifying which spouse's income acquired the property if a title is irrelevant. In the last decade,

2   "The Common Law and Civil Law Traditions," The Robbins Collection, University of California at Berkeley, School of Law (Boalt Hall) (2010): 1–4, at https://www.law.berkeley.edu/library/robbins/CommonLawCivilLawTraditions.html (last accessed March 15, 2018).

3   Luis Acosta, "United States: Inheritance Laws in the 19th and 20th Centuries," Library of Congress, at https://www.loc.gov/law/help/inheritance-laws/unitedstates.php (last updated June 9, 2015).

states have increased the protection of the surviving spouse through the augmentation of elective share rights that guarantee a certain portion of the decedent's estate, a testament to the contrary notwithstanding. Inheritance law generally lets the surviving spouse claim at least one-third of the deceased spouse's property. Some states also allow children of the deceased to claim an elective share.[4] These elective share rights derive from the English common law concepts of dower and curtesy.[5]

On June 25, 2015, the Basque Autonomous Community passed the 5/2015 Basque Civil Law repealing the 3/1992 Foral Civil Law, which falls within its exclusive competences, as Article 10.5 of the Basque Statute of Autonomy states. Spanish civil law is a supplementary source when necessary. This new law regulates the Basque inheritance system, which is mainly customary and based on the Old law but updated for our times and establishes a Basque civil residence (*vecindad civil vasca*).[6] It also reduces children's legitimacy to one third of the total estate, increasing testamentary freedom and the protection of surviving spouses. The only exception is the Charter of Ayala (*Fuero de Ayala*),[7] which stipulates complete testamentary freedom.

This law also extends testamentary power (*poder testatorio*)[8] to all of the Basque Autonomous Community, when it was originally only used in Bizkaia. Testamentary power is a delegation to attest. The testator delegates the heirs' election to the commissioner (*comisario*), usually the surviving spouse. The commissioner chooses the inheritors and decides on the distribution of the estate. Spouses usually designate each other as commissioner and beneficial owner, therefore, when one of them dies, the surviving spouse is protected and will make all the decisions in relation to the estate of the deceased spouse. This is called *alkar poderoso*.

---

4   Ronald J. Scalise Jr., "New Developments in Succession Law: The US Report," *Electronic Journal of Comparative Law* 14, no. 2 (October 2010), 4–9.
5   The rights of dower and curtesy originated in early England. They stipulated that the surviving spouse had a right in the estate and a means of support after the death of a spouse. Dower was a widow's right to one-third of the life estate in the property of her husband during the marriage and curtesy was the right of a widower to a life estate in all real property of his wife at the time of marriage, only if the issue of the marriage were born alive. Practically all states have repealed dower and curtesy and have enacted a statutory elective share instead. "Creation of Dower and Curtesy Right or Interest," US Legal, at https://dowerandcourtesy.uslegal.com/creation-of-dower-and-courtesy-right-or-interest/.
6   Articles 10–11 and Seventh Transitional Provision.
7   Articles 88–95.
8   Articles 30–46.

Another important tool for estate planning is the agreement to succession (*pacto sucesorio*).[9] In this case, the grantor, that is, the property owner, designates as heir someone of his/her liking in a contract between him/her and the grantor with some legal burdens and conditions for the inheritor. This contract can be related to a part of the inheritance or to all of it. The property can be transferred to the heir before or after (*post mortem*) the death of the grantor. A testamentary contract invalidates a previous will and can only be modified by a new agreement between them or their successors or as result of any reason described in the initial contract.

Estate planning in the United States is very important in order to avoid probate, a public and long court process to determine the deceased's estate distribution. The most important tools for estate planning are trusts. Whereas there are different types of trusts depending on their purposes, the basic categories are revocable and irrevocable. In a revocable or living trust, the grantor generally maintains the power to modify or revoke the trust, while in an irrevocable trust the grantor cannot revoke it once the trust is created. As it is irrevocable, it is not part of the estate. The grantor sets up a trust, which is managed by the trustee following the orders established by the grantor, in order to benefit the beneficiary.[10] Trustees have the bare legal property of the trust. They also have a fiduciary duty to beneficiaries, among other responsibilities. Beneficiaries are the owners of the benefices of the trust but they do not own the trust property. Therefore, they can use it and profit from it but they cannot sell the trust property or rent it. Trusts can be created during a person's lifetime and survive the person's death but they cannot last forever by virtue of the rule against perpetuities, "a common law property rule that states that no interest in land is good unless it must vest, if at all, not later than twenty-one years after the death of some life in being at the creation of the interest."[11] Since the meaning of this rule is virtually impossible to decipher, many states have modified it,

---

9   Articles 100–109.

10   Cathy Pareto, "Estate Planning: Introduction to Trusts," Investopedia, at https://www.investopedia.com/university/estate-planning/estate-planning6.asp#ixzz5EZPtPJPk.

11   Cornell Law School, at https://www.law.cornell.edu/wex/rule_against_perpetuities.

like in Nevada where it terminates within 365 years after its creation,[12] and some others have abolished it altogether, like in South Dakota.[13]

When a trust is created, the grantor has to submit the gift tax refund and use its exemptions, which will be explained later. In summary, the main reasons to settle up a trust are to avoid probate and guardianship when the grantor becomes mentally incapacitated, to manage and protect assets, or to control distributions and protect children's wealth in case they are not mature enough to manage all the estate when the grantor dies, among other reasons.[14]

Concerning the Basque Autonomous Community, the original aims of the different estate tools were to preserve the family property and to transfer its entirety to the best inheritor. Nowadays, the main goal is to get better protection for the surviving spouse in the case of testamentary power, and better estate planning for the family business can be achieved by using the agreement for succession, even though it is a lesser-known tool.

WEALTH TRANSFER TAXES IN THE UNITED STATES

The US Constitution created a federal system of government in which power is distributed between the federal government and the state governments. Because of that, states diverge widely in their laws and institutions, showing differences in social values. This diversity among states is reflected in state taxation as well.

Gratuitous transfers of property are taxable through three different taxes in the United States: through the estate tax, the gift tax, and the generation-skipping transfer tax. These taxes are collected by the federal government, although states can approve their own wealth transfer taxes. These three taxes are also connected to each other by a lifetime exemption of $5.49 million per person in 2017, and $11.18 million in the period 2018–2025 under the Tax Cut and Jobs Act approved on December 22, 2017, during President Trump's term in office. The exemptions have been

---

12 2010 Nevada Code Title 10 Property Rights and Transactions Chapter 111 Estates in Property; Conveyancing and Recording NRS 111.1031 Statutory rule against perpetuities.

13 2012 South Dakota Codified Laws Title 43 Property Chapter 05. Restraints on Alienation of Property §43-5-8 Rule against perpetuities not in force.

14 G. Barton Mowry, attorney at law in Reno, Nevada, interviewed by the author, May 4, 2018.

increased throughout the last years ($1,500,000 in the period 2004–2005; $2,000,000 in the period 2006–2008; $3,500,000 in 2009; $5,000,000 in the period 2010–2011; $5,120,000 in 2012, $5,250,000 in 2013, $5,340,000 in 2014, $5,430,000 in 2015, and $5,450,000 in 2016).[15]

ESTATE TAX AND INHERITANCE TAX

The estate tax is a tax on property transfers due to death. It consists of an accounting of everything the deceased person owned at the date of death, using the fair market value of these items. Estate taxes are levied on the net value of an estate, after exclusions or credits. Estates of decedents survived by a spouse may elect to pass any of the deceased's unused exemption to the surviving spouse. Family-owned farms and closely-held businesses can decrease the tax or prolong payments over time thanks to special provisions. Estates that accomplish certain requirements can reduce the taxable value of their real estate, frequently by 40 to 70 percent, and if a business or a farm is no less than 35 percent of the gross estate value, the tax can be paid by installments over fourteen years at reduced interest rates, paying interests only during the first four years, and then a tenth of the tax and the remaining interest during the last ten years.[16]

Inheritance taxes are paid by successors based on their portion of the inheritance and, often, their relationship with the decedent. While estate taxes are paid by the deceased's estate before assets are distributed to heirs, inheritance taxes are paid by the receiver of a bequest. Both taxes exempt transfers made to the surviving spouse.

For years, there was a credit against federal estate tax for state inheritance and estate taxes paid. This allowed states to levy a "pick-up" estate tax without increasing residents' total tax liability. This credit was eliminated in 2005 and a deduction took its place. This deduction is far less generous than the previous credit. Because of that, states started an estate and inheritance tax competition among them to decrease these taxes and become more attractive to residents, which is likely to continue.

As already mentioned, the federal estate tax includes a "unified credit" that functionally eliminates burden under an exempted amount,

---

15   Internal Revenue Service (IRS), "Estate tax," at https://www.irs.gov/businesses/small-businesses-self-employed/estate-tax.
16   Tax Policy Center, *Briefing Book,* at http://www.taxpolicycenter.org/briefing-book/how-do-estate-gift-and-generation-skipping-transfer-taxes-work.

currently $11,180,000. It is also portable between spouses, meaning that the deceased spouse's unused exclusion amount may be used by the surviving spouse. All estate value above that threshold is taxed at the top marginal rate, currently 40 percent. Some states' rates equal the federal exemption, whereas others adopt their own exemptions and exclusions. The most common structure used by the states is an exemption amount rather than a credit against liability, which eliminates taxation of income below a certain amount but removes the lower tax brackets.

Twelve states and the District of Colombia have an estate tax and six states impose an inheritance tax. Maryland is the only state in the country to levy both of them. New Jersey had both taxes until 2017 when the estate tax was repealed from 2018 on, as it was in Delaware.

Does Your State Have An Estate or Inheritance Tax?

State Estate & Inheritance Tax Rates & Exemptions in 2018

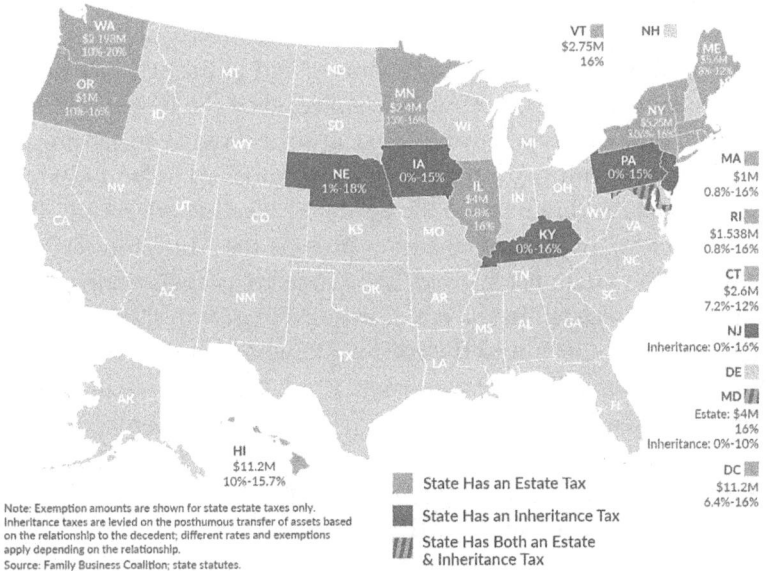

Note: Exemption amounts are shown for state estate taxes only. Inheritance taxes are levied on the posthumous transfer of assets based on the relationship to the decedent; different rates and exemptions apply depending on the relationship.
Source: Family Business Coalition; state statutes.

State Has an Estate Tax
State Has an Inheritance Tax
State Has Both an Estate & Inheritance Tax

TAX FOUNDATION   @TaxFoundation

Source: Tax Foundation.

See https://files.taxfoundation.org/20180417165034/EstateTax-2018-01.png.

Inheritance taxes usually have distinct rate schedules for different classes of inheritors. Relatives receive favored treatment compared to nonrelated persons, and direct lineal descendants sometimes are exempted. Unlike estate taxes, inheritance taxes generally do not offer large exemptions.

States also apply different deductions and rules to determine the fair market value for tax purposes. Some states follow all federal deductions, while others approve their own or none. Most states have assumed the Uniform Simultaneous Death Act, which establishes that if two or more people die within a short time (120 hours) of each other in the same accident and there are no wills, assets are transferred directly to relatives without first being transmitted from one estate to the other. State top rates for estate taxes range from 12 percent in Connecticut and Maine to 20 percent in Washington State. Another important difference between federal and state estate taxes is that usually there is no portability between spouses at the state level.[17]

Maryland, the only state that levies both estate and inheritance taxes, imposes a flat rate inheritance tax of 10 percent on all beneficiaries other than lineal inheritors. Therefore, spouses and lineal heirs are exempt from the inheritance tax. This tax is collected by the Register of Wills situated in the county where the decedent either lived or owned property. Then, that amount is subtracted from the gross Maryland estate tax liability and the difference is the estate tax owed to Maryland. If the inheritance tax payment matches or exceeds the Maryland estate tax, no Maryland estate tax is owed. The estate tax is apportioned among all persons interested in the estate proportionately to the value of the interest of each person to the total value, as Md. Tax-General Code Ann. § 7-308 establishes. According to legislation approved in 2014, the Maryland estate tax exemption, which is not portable between spouses until it matches the federal exclusion amount, has been augmented to $4,000,000 (an increase of $1,000,000 from 2017) and it will equal the federal exception amount in 2019 and thereafter.[18]

---

17 Jared Walczak, "State Inheritance and Estate Taxes: Rates, Economic Implications, and the Return of Interstate Competition," *Tax Foundation* (July 2017): 3–8, at https://files.taxfoundation.org/20171024103443/Tax-Foundation-SR2351.pdf.

18 Revenue Administration Division of Maryland, "What You Need to Know About Maryland's Estate Tax," at http://taxes.marylandtaxes.gov/Resource_Library/Tax_Publications/Tax_Tips/Personal_Tax_Tips/tip42.pdf.

GIFT TAX

The gift tax is a tax on property transfers donated by one person to another while obtaining nothing, or less than full value in return. Since 1977, estate and gift taxes have worked as a unified tax at the federal level, with lifetime donations deducted from the federal estate tax exemption. The gift tax is the liability of the donor and the amount of tax due is based on the gift value. According to the current law, property received by lifetime gift from a donor generally takes a carryover basis, which means that the basis in the hands of the donee is the same as it was in the hands of the donor, increased by any gift tax paid by the donor, although never above fair market value. However, property obtained from a deceased's estate generally takes a stepped-up basis, meaning the fair market value on the date of the deceased's death.

The federal annual exemption applied to gifts donated to each donee was $11,000 in the period 2002–2005, $12,000 in the period 2006–2008, $13,000 in the period 2009–2012, and $14,000 in the period 2013–2017. For 2018, the annual exclusion is $15,000. There are also educational and medical exemptions, although the payments must be made directly to the educational or medical institution in order to qualify for the exclusion. Transfers between spouses are not considered gifts, no matter the amount, and neither are gifts to a political organization. In addition to this, donations to qualifying charities are deductible from the value of the gifts made.[19]

Connecticut is the only state with a state gift tax. In 2017, the gift and the estate taxes were repealed and replaced by the estate and gift tax, which connects both taxes. The donor is allowed an annual exclusion of $10,000 per donee.[20] The Connecticut State budget signed on October 31, 2017, increased the individual exemption from $2,000,000 up to $2,600,000 in 2018, to $3,600,000 in 2019, and to match the federal estate and gift tax exemption in 2020. The maximum quantity of gift and estate tax paid by donors or estates of residents and nonresidents who die on or after January 1, 2016 is $20 million. This quantity is reduced by the amount of any gift taxes paid by the decedent, the decedent's estate,

---

19 IRS, "Frequently Asked Questions on Gift Taxes," at https://www.irs.gov/businesses/small-businesses-self-employed/frequently-asked-questions-on-gift-taxes.
20 Department of Revenue Services, "A Guide to the Federal and Connecticut Gift Taxes," at http://www.ct.gov/drs/cwp/view.asp?A=1510&Q=266934.

or the decedent's spouse on or after January 1, 2016. Public Act 17-2 (JSS) reduces the payment cap to $15 million for estates of deceased dying on or after January 1, 2019.[21]

GENERATION-SKIPPING TRANSFER TAX

The generation-skipping transfer tax (GST) is a federal tax on a transfer of property that skips a generation. Congress passed the GST tax in 1976 to stop families from avoiding the estate tax by making gifts or bequests directly to grandchildren or great-grandchildren. The GST tax uses the exemption and the top tax rate of the estate tax on wealth transfers to receivers who are two or more generations younger than the donor. No state levies a GST.

COMPARISON BETWEEN THE BASQUE AUTONOMOUS COMMUNITY AND THE US FISCAL SYSTEMS

Financial and tax relations between the Basque Country and the Spanish state are set up by the Economic Agreement, which confers tax powers to these three Basque provinces. The *foral* governments collect almost all taxes. In other words, the Spanish state does not collect the agreed taxes in the Basque Autonomous Community. This is, without any doubt, the main difference between the Basque and the US fiscal systems.[22]

The Inheritance and Gift tax in the Basque Autonomous Community is an agreed tax approved by the Historical Territories of Bizkaia, Araba, and Gipuzkoa. In other words, there are three regulations, one in each territory of the Basque Country, which rule this tax. In the Basque Autonomous Community there is neither an estate tax nor GST. The gift tax is paid by the donee, unlike in the United States where the donor is the taxpayer. Inheritance and gift taxes are ruled by the same regulation, with different rates depending on the relationship between the deceased and beneficiary or donor and donee. These rates range from 1.5 to 42.56 percent. A reduction of €400,000 is applied when

---

21 State of Connecticut Department of Revenue Services, *Fiscal Year 2016–17 Annual Report*, 5, 10, 43–44, 78.

22 The Economic Agreement is governed by Law 12/2002, of May 23, by which the Economic Agreement of the Autonomous Community of the Basque Country was approved.

the heir is the surviving spouse, registered partnership, or direct lineal descendant or ascendant, and smaller reductions are applied if there is a different form of kinship. Among others, there are reductions linked to the family business or to a habitual dwelling, as well as some small differences among the three regulations.

Briefly, the biggest differences between Basque and US taxes are with respect to the value of the gift received by the donee. In the United States this is calculated on a carryover basis and the tax is paid by the donor, while in the Basque Country it takes the fair market value and the donee pays the tax. Moreover, in the Basque Country, when the gift is not just money, there could be a gain the donor would have to declare in his or her personal income tax. That gain is the difference between the fair market value of the donation day and the price paid when that gift was bought, updated to the day of the donation.[23] This does not happen in the United States.[24]

Therefore, any inheritance received in the Basque Country valued at more than €400,000, in the best-case scenario, will have to pay the pertinent tax, whereas the exempted amount in the federal estate tax is $11,180,000 so there would be no tax to pay if the exemption is not used up. In the case of a donation, there is no exemption in the Basque tax system, while the federal gift tax allows an annual exclusion of $15,000 per donee plus the general exclusion of $11,180,000.

In consequence, it can be said that wealth transfer taxes are only paid by the wealthiest people in the United States. Estate tax income has decreased in recent years, and its share of total federal revenue is down from about 1 percent in 1990 to 0.7 percent.[25] It will be even less in the future as the exemption in 2018 was doubled. Moreover, estate and inheritance taxes collected 0.7 percent of the total revenues according to the 2017 Comprehensive Annual Financial Report of Maryland, and a 1.3 percent in Connecticut along with its Department of Revenue Services.

---

23 Governed by articles 40–50 of Foral Decree 13/2013, of December 5, on Personal Income Tax, Historical Territory of Bizkaia; by articles 40–50 of Foral Decree 33/2013, of November 27, on Personal Income Tax, Historical Territory of Araba; and by articles 40–50 of Foral Decree 3/2014, of January 17, on Personal Income Tax, Historical Territory of Gipuzkoa.
24 Mowry, interview, May 4, 2018.
25 Office of Management and Budget, Historical Tables, at https://www.whitehouse.gov/omb/budget/Historicals.

On the other hand, 6.2 percent of the agreed tax revenues were raised by these taxes in the Basque Autonomous Community,[26] although it must be said that until 2012, gratuitous wealth transfers between spouses or to direct lineal descendants or ascendants were exempt from these taxes. The exemption was eliminated due to the crisis.

Regarding allocating factors, the Economic Agreement establishes specific rules for each agreed tax. In this case, Article 25[27] determines that the Inheritance and Gift tax will be levied by the foral government territorially competent when the decedent's or donee's tax residence is in the Basque Autonomous Community on the date of the accrual of the tax. If the decedent's tax residence is abroad, the tax will be levied by the foral governments if the taxpayer's residence is in the Basque Autonomous Community, as well as if a Basque real property is donated. If the largest value of the assets is located in the Basque Country or if a life insurance contract was hired with an insurance company residing in the Basque territory for tax purposes or signed by a foreign insurance company in the Basque Autonomous Community, the tax will be collected by the

---

26   Economy and Tax Office of the Government of the Basque Autonomous
     Community, at http://www.euskadi.eus/recaudacion/web01-s2oga/es/.
27   Article 25 states: "Applicable legislation and levying of the Tax. One. The
     Inheritance and Gift Tax is an agreed tax subject to autonomous legislation. It shall
     be levied by the foral government territorially competent in the following cases:
     a) In 'mortis causa' acquisitions income received by life insurance beneficiaries,
     when the decedent's tax residence is in the Basque Autonomous Community
     on the date of the accrual of the tax. If the decedent has his/her tax residence
     abroad, when the taxpayers are resident in the Basque Autonomous Community.
     b) In gifts or donations of real property and rights on them, when the property
     is located in the Basque territory. If the real property is abroad, when the donee's
     habitual residence is the Basque Autonomous Community on the date of the
     accrual of the tax. For the purposes of the provision in this subsection b), gratuitous
     transfers of securities referred to in article 108 of Royal Legislative Decree
     4/2015, October 23, approving the consolidated text of the Securities Market
     Law, shall be considered donations of real property. c) In any other gifts of assets
     or rights, when the donee's habitual residence is in the Basque Autonomous
     Community on the date of the accrual of the tax. d) If the taxpayer has his/her tax
     residence abroad, when the biggest value of the assets or rights is located in the
     Basque Autonomous Community; as well as with the income derived from life
     insurance contracts, when contracts are signed by insurance entities residing for
     tax purposes in the Basque territory, or when contracts are signed in the Basque
     Autonomous Community by foreign entities operating therein. For the purposes
     of this subsection d), it will be deemed that assets and rights are located in the
     Basque territory, when they are sited, may be exercised or must be fulfilled therein.
     Two. In the cases referred to in subsections a) and c) of the above section, the
     foral governments shall apply the regulations of the common territory when the
     decedent or the donee had lived in the common territory most days in the previous
     5 years to the date the accrual of the tax. This rule shall not apply to people who
     keep the political status of Basque according to Article 7º.2 of the Statute of
     Autonomy." Translated by Gemma Martínez Bárbara and the author.

foral governments when the taxpayer is a nonresident for tax purposes. In all other cases, the tax will be levied by the Spanish government.

Tax harmonization between the Basque Autonomous Community and the Spanish state is established by Article 41.2[28] of the Basque Statute of Autonomy, which lays down the principles and guidelines the Economic Agreement has to respect, and by Article 2 (general principles)[29] and Article 3 (fiscal harmonization)[30] of the Economic Agreement.

---

28 Article 41.2 states: "The content of the Agreement regime shall respect and be adapted to the following principles and guidelines: a) The competent Institutions of the Historic Territories may maintain, establish and regulate, within their own territory, the tax system, bearing in mind the general tax structure of the State, the rules container in the Economic Agreement itself for co-ordination, fiscal harmonization and collaboration with the State, and those to be issued by the Basque Parliament for the same purposes within the Autonomous Community. The Economic Agreement shall be approved by law. b) The levying, management, demand, collection and inspection of all taxes, except those included in the Customs Revenue and those currently collected by means of Tax Monopolies, shall be carried out, within each Historic Territory, by the respective Provincial Councils, without prejudice to collaboration with the State and its inspection service. c) The competent institutions of the Historic Territories shall adopt the relevant agreements, with the object of applying within their respective territories whatever exceptional or provisional tax rules the State may decide to enforce in the ordinary territory...."

29 Article 2 states: "General principles. One. The taxation system established by the Historical Territories shall be in accordance with the following principles: First. Respect for the principle of solidarity in the terms laid down in the Constitution and in the Statute of Autonomy. Second. Regard for the general taxation structure of the State. Third. Coordination, fiscal harmonization and cooperation with the State, in accordance with the rules laid down in the present Economic Agreement. Fourth. Coordination, fiscal harmonization and mutual cooperation between the Institutions of the Historical Territories pursuant to the regulations enacted by the Basque Parliament for these purposes. Fifth. Submission to the International Agreements or Treaties signed and ratified or adhered to by the Spanish State. In particular, it shall comply with the provisions laid down in the International Agreements signed by Spain to avoid double taxation, as well as fiscal harmonization measures of the European Union, and shall be responsible for making the refunds called for, pursuant to application of said Agreements and rules. Two. The rules laid down herein shall be interpreted in accordance with the provisions contained in the General Tax Law for the interpretation of tax regulations."

30 Article 3 states: "Fiscal harmonization. In drafting their tax legislation, the Historical Territories shall: a) Respect the General Tax Law in matters of terminology and concepts, a) without prejudice to the peculiarities established in the present Economic Agreement. b) Maintain an overall effective fiscal pressure equivalent to that in force in b) the rest of the State. Respect and guarantee freedom of movement and establishment of persons and the free movement of goods, capital and services throughout the territory of Spain, without giving rise to discrimination or a lessening of the possibilities of commercial competition or to distortion in the allocation of resources. d) Use the same system for classifying livestock, mining, industrial, commercial, service, professional and artistic activities as is used in the so-called common territory, without prejudice to further itemizations that might be made."

To resolve conflicts between the Spanish state and the foral governments, the Economic Agreement sets up the Board of Arbitration,[31] made up of three members appointed and formalized by the Spanish Minister of Finance and Public Administrations and the Basque Minister of Treasury and Finance. One of its main functions is to resolve disputes over the application of the allocating factors for the agreed taxes arising between these administrations. The resolutions of the Board of Arbitration can be appealed before the Supreme Court.

On the other hand, on September 3, 2014, the Court of Justice of the European Union declared that "the Kingdom of Spain has failed to fulfil its obligations under Article 63[32] of the Treaty on the Functioning of the European Union (TFEU) and Article 40[33] of the Agreement on the European Economic Area of 2 May 1992," when "applying different tax treatment to donations and successions between beneficiaries and donees resident in Spain and those not resident in Spain, between bequeathers resident in Spain and those not resident in Spain, and between donations and similar transfers of immovable property situated within and outside of Spain."[34] Because of this sentence, the Spanish Inheritance and Gift tax[35] was amended to eliminate those discriminations. Article 25 of the Economic Agreement was amended too,[36] after the agreement signed by the Joint Committee on the Economic Agreement on July 19, 2017,[37]

---

31 Articles 65–67 of the Economic Agreement.
32 Article 63 TFEU states: "1. Within the framework of the provisions set out in this Chapter, all restrictions on the movement of capital between Member States and between Member States and third countries shall be prohibited. 2. Within the framework of the provisions set out in this Chapter, all restrictions on payments between Member States and between Member States and third countries shall be prohibited."
33 Article 40 states: "Within the framework of the provisions of this Agreement, there shall be no restrictions between the Contracting Parties on the movement of capital belonging to persons resident in EC Member States or EFTA States and no discrimination based on the nationality or on the place of residence of the parties or on the place where such capital is invested. Annex XII contains the provisions necessary to implement this Article."
34 Case C-127/12.
35 Law 29/1987, of December 18, on the Tax on Inheritances and Donations.
36 Law 10/2017, of December 28, modifying Law 12/2002, of May 23, by which the Economic Agreement of the Autonomous Community of the Basque Country was approved.
37 The Joint Committee on the Economic Agreement is the highest relation committee between the Spanish administration and the Basque administration, and in addition to the specific duties assigned by the law, exercises any and all agreements involving matters of tax and finance deemed necessary at any given time for the correct application and development of the provisions contained in the Economic Agreement. The Joint Committee is made up of twelve members, six representatives of the central administration, and the same number of representatives of the Basque administration. See http://www.conciertoeconomico.

to include the collection of the inheritance and gift tax by the foral governments when it concerns nonresident decedents, nonresident donees, donations of Basque real property, and nonresident beneficiaries of life insurances contracted in the Basque Autonomous Community.

Out of the tax scope and for the purposes of harmonization in the European Union, Regulation (EU) No. 650/2012 of the European Parliament and of the Council of July 4, 2012, must be mentioned. This Regulation shall apply to succession to the estates of deceased persons but does not interfere with the fiscal regulation on each estate. Articles 21 and 22 establish that "the law applicable to the succession as a whole shall be the law of the State in which the deceased had his habitual residence at the time of death," except "the deceased was manifestly more closely connected with a State other" or had chosen "the law of the State whose nationality he possessed at the time of making the choice or at the time of death."

As far as the United States are concerned, the federal taxes will always be levied by the federal government if the decedent or donor is a US citizen or resident, or in the case of nonresidents, if the decedent had US-situated assets or if a tangible property located in the United States is donated.[38]

With regard to state taxes, in Connecticut the gift tax is to be paid by resident donors and by nonresident individuals when the donated property is located in Connecticut or if it is employed in carrying out trade or business within Connecticut. The Connecticut estate tax is required when the deceased was domiciled in Connecticut at the time of death or when real or tangible personal property in Connecticut was owned by a nonresident decedent.[39] In Maryland, estate and inheritance taxes are collected when the deceased was a resident of Maryland at the date of death or a nonresident who owned real or tangible personal property that has a taxable situs in Maryland.[40] Consequently and

---

org/en/for-students-and-professionals/detailed-study-of-the-agreement/committees/the-joint-committe-on-the-economic-agreement, Ad Concordiam.

38 IRS, last updated April 13, 2018. See https://www.irs.gov/businesses/small-businesses-self-employed/frequently-asked-questions-on-estate-taxes and https://www.irs.gov/pub/irs-pdf/i709.pdf.

39 State of Connecticut, Department of Revenue Services, "A Guide to the Federal and Connecticut Gift Taxes," at http://www.ct.gov/drs/cwp/view.asp?A=1510&Q=266934.

40 Peter, Franchot, Comptroller of Maryland, "What You Need to Know about Maryland's Estate Tax," at http://taxes.marylandtaxes.gov/Resource_Library/Tax_Publications/Tax_Tips/Personal_Tax_Tips/tip42.pdf.

generally speaking, taxes will be paid to the state where the taxpayer´s residence is except for those taxes linked to a real property that will be paid to the state where the real property is located.[41]

If an issue is not resolved through administrative proceedings, a taxpayer can file suit in federal court or in a state court, depending on the issue. When the disagreement is between states, it will be resolved by the US Supreme Court which has the original jurisdiction in all cases when a state is Party, according to Article III of the US Constitution.

Consequently, harmonization is much more complex in the Basque Autonomous Community than in the United States due to its multi-level harmonization system; in other words, harmonization among the three Historical Territories, harmonization between the Basque Country and the Spanish government; and, lastly, harmonization among the countries of the European Union. In the United States however, there is less of a need for harmonization, considering that it is only supposed to be among states and most of them lack any wealth transfer tax.

HISTORICAL BACKGROUND AND FUTURE OF WEALTH TRANSFER TAXES

In the United States, wealth transfer taxes were initially enacted to finance an imminent or actual war and revoked once these revenue needs had passed, as happened in 1797, 1862, 1898, and 1916, but this last time the current estate tax, introduced because of World War I, became permanent. In 1924, the federal government activated a federal credit for state inheritance and estate taxes. Accordingly, many states changed their old inheritance taxes into estate taxes after the federal model. The Economic Growth Tax Relief Reconciliation Act of 2001 (also called the first Bush tax cut) included a four-year phase-out of that credit, swapping it with a much less generous tax deduction by 2005. As a result, some states repealed their estate and inheritance taxes, others technically maintained them but zero rated, and a smaller number of states kept some kind of wealth taxation.[42]

In Spain, these taxes appeared at the end of the eighteenth century. During the nineteenth century, they were repealed, enacted, and modified

---

41 Mowry, interview, May 4, 2018.
42 Walczak, "State Inheritance and Estate Taxes," 8.

several times. Succeeding the reestablishment of democracy, a major tax reform was approved. After that, significant changes occurred when the Basque territories approved an exemption on bequests to direct lineal relatives in the 1990s within the powers conferred by the Economic Agreement, and when the collection of these taxes was transferred to the rest of the Spanish regions subject to the common system of financing in 1996. This last fact resulted in the near disappearance of these taxes in some of these autonomous communities.

In 2014, a report from the Tax Reform Expert Commission, requested by the Spanish government, was published. This report said that the inheritance and gift tax should be maintained in order to improve equal opportunities and the fairness of the tax system, and because taxing inheritances can encourage daily effort and daily work. They also proposed some modifications to achieve a greater harmonization among the autonomous communities.[43]

In the same way, in 2015 in the United States, the Joint Committee on Taxation presented a document describing some proposals to modify the taxation of wealth transfers. The most important ones were to repeal the estate and generation-skipping transfer taxes, to expand the taxation of wealth transfers by decreasing exemption amounts and increasing tax rates, to expand the transfer tax base, and to impose a new tax on the transfer of built-in gains at the time of a gift or upon a decedent's death.[44] Some of the proposals to expand the tax base were to require a minimum term for grantor retained annuity trusts, or to limit the generation-skipping transfer tax exemption for dynasty trusts. But we must remember that document was presented during Barack Obama's time in office, and now the United States is governed by a Republican government.

The last report about world inequality says that global wealth inequality has risen over the past decades. Wealth is becoming more concentrated in the United States too, with the top 10 percent of the population owning over 77 percent of all US wealth in 2012, which is more than three quarters of it. In Spain, the top 10 percent owned almost 57 percent of Spain's personal wealth in 2013.[45]

---

43 Comisión de Expertos para la Reforma del Sistema Tributario Español, *Informe*, February 2014, 10, 218, 248–49.

44 Joint Committee on Taxation, "History, Present Law, and Analysis of the Federal Wealth Transfer Tax System," (JCX-52-15) (March 16, 2015), 47.

45 Facundo Alvaredo, Lucas Chancel, Thomas Piketty, Emmanuel Saez, and Gabriel Zucman, *World Inequality Report 2018* (Paris: World Inequality Lab, 2017), 212–

A considerable share of actual wealth is indeed inherited. Excessive concentrations of wealth can threaten democratic institutions, social stability, and economic growth, since extreme disparities in the distribution of inherited wealth lead to political and economic power perpetuation from one generation to the next. Wealth transfer taxes can curb extreme concentrations of wealth, help with the equitable distribution of the tax burden, regulate the intergenerational transmission of wealth, as well as raise revenue.

Despite conferring these functions to wealth transfer taxes, some experts present other alternatives to the gift and estate tax, such as an annual wealth tax, taxing unrealized gains, taxing gifts and inheritances as income or the lifetime accessions tax. The reason is that these taxes are deeply unpopular as a result of an "anti-death tax" campaign, and, in the case of the United States, because these taxes are applied to donors rather than donees and therefore easily considered as a double taxation on hardworking donors.[46]

Voices in the United States against these taxes appeal to the low revenue collected by them, the high cost of estate and inheritance tax avoidance, and cash flow burdens on small or family-owned business, among other arguments. Republicans are openly in favor of repealing them, arguing in part that it will protect millions of small businesses and the American farmer. Donald Trump said he would repeal the estate tax while campaigning to become president, but he has not done it yet. Some Republicans are angry because they think the estate tax will not disappear in 2025, and it will rise back to what it was before its last reform. Democrats, on the other hand, would maintain these taxes and they think the increase of the exemption amount is far too much.

As taxes are settled in a political context, politicians are affected not only by economic guidance but also by the voters' opinions and by special interest groups. In Spain, the PP party defends the disappearance of these taxes when it governs autonomous communities, but they have not been repealed during this party's term in office in the Spanish government. Currently, not a single party stands up for its elimination, but almost all the most important parties defend a bigger exemption

---

14, 230–33.
46   David G. Duff, "Alternatives to the Gift and Estate Tax," *Boston College Law Review* 57 (2016), 7–11.

and the harmonization of the lower tax rates among autonomous communities.[47]

CONCLUSION

A good tax system must be fair and consistent with the country´s social values, like equal opportunities or social progress. Progressiveness by imposing a higher tax burden on those with a greater capacity to pay can help to achieve a fairer world. Nevertheless, income inequality has increased in nearly all countries in the last decades. One of the reasons for this increase is the inheritance wealth, which is becoming significantly larger. On the other hand, governments have become poorer because of the growth of public debt, which has reached almost 100 percent of national income in most industrialized economies. Historically, there are three different ways to reduce large public debts: progressive taxes on capital, debt relief, and inflation. As inflation is hard to control, a combination of the other two policies seems to be more appropriate.[48]

Although many experts consider wealth transfer taxes as a way to combat inequality of opportunities through their contribution to the progressiveness of the tax system, these taxes continue to be extremely unpopular and politically vulnerable. Critics claim that wealth transfer taxes discourage capital accumulation and economic growth, even though empirical studies suggest that these taxes have relatively little influence on the magnitude of wealth transfers. Moreover, their minor role in the revenue system is another argument used to criticize them. For all these reasons, many experts have proposed different alternatives to gift and estate taxation. However, despite the need for revenue, the contribution of these taxes to tax burden equitability, and their capacity to curb extreme concentrations of wealth,[49] it is also possible that political considerations and pressures become more important when deciding on their future. Therefore, time will tell what happens with them.

---

47 Marina Estévez, "Esto es lo que harán los partidos con los impuestos de Sucesiones y Patrimonio," *El Diario*, February 9, 2018, at https://www.eldiario.es/economia/pretenden-impuestos-Sucesiones-Patrimonio-electorales_0_738426723.html.

48 Alvaredo, Chancel, Piketty, Saez, and Zucman, *World Inequality Report 2018*, 36, 280–81.

49 Duff, "Alternatives," 3, 5–8.

BIBLIOGRAPHY

Acosta, Luis. "United States: Inheritance Laws in the 19th and 20th Centuries." *Library of Congress*, last modified June 9, 2015. At https://www.loc.gov/law/help/inheritance-laws/unitedstates.php.

Alvaredo, Facundo, Lucas Chancel, Thomas Piketty, Emmanuel Saez, and Gabriel Zucman. *World Inequality Report 2018*. Paris: World Inequality Lab, 2017. At http://wir2018.wid.world/files/download/wir2018-full-report-english.pdf.

Comisión de Expertos para la Reforma del Sistema Tributario Español. *Informe*. Madrid, February 2014. At http://www.abc.es/gestordocumental/uploads/economia/fe007a24af859ec8ce-790387ba6b7755.pdf.

Duff, David G. "Alternatives to the Gift and Estate Tax." *Boston College Law Review* 57, no. 3, March 26, 2016. At http://lawdigitalcommons.bc.edu/bclr/vol57/iss3/8.

Griffin, Joseph M. "State of Maryland Register of Wills for Montgomery County, Maryland." September 8, 2014. At http://registers.maryland.gov/main/region/montgomery/Probate%20Policies%20and%20Procedures%202014.pdf.

Joint Committee on Taxation. "History, Present Law, and Analysis of the Federal Wealth Transfer Tax System." JCX-52-15, March 16, 2015.

Pareto, Cathy. "Estate Planning: Introduction to Trusts." *Investopedia*. At https://www.investopedia.com/university/estate-planning/estate-planning6.asp#ixzz5EZPtPJPk.

The Robbins Collection, University of California, Berkeley, School of Law. "The Common Law and Civil Law Traditions," 1–4. At https://www.law.berkeley.edu/library/robbins/CommonLaw-CivilLawTraditions.html.

Scalise, Ronald J., Jr. "New Developments in Succession Law: The US Report." *Electronic Journal of Comparative Law* 14, no. 2 (October 2010): 4–9. At https://www.ejcl.org/142/art142-5.pdf.

State of Connecticut Department of Revenue Services. *Fiscal Year 2016–17 Annual Report*. At http://www.ct.gov/drs/lib/drs/research/annualreport/drs_fy17_annual_report.pdf.

Tax Policy Center. *Briefing Book*. At http://www.taxpolicycenter.org/ briefing-book/how-do-estate-gift-and-generation-skipping-transfer-taxes-work.

Walczak, Jared. "State Inheritance and Estate Taxes: Rates, Economic Implications, and the Return of Interstate Competition." *Tax Foundation*, Special Report No. 235 (July 2017): 3–8. At https:// files.taxfoundation.org/20171024103443/Tax-Foundation-SR2351.pdf.

Chapter 5

The Basque and Swiss Fiscal Systems Building Processes as a Source of Lessons for the European Integration Process

Mikel Erkoreka Gonzalez

Now that the worst of the 2007 crisis seems to have been overcome, European institutions have opened up a period of reflection in order to discuss the reforms needed to achieve an improved performance of the European Union (EU). In this connection, several proposals for the future of the EU multilevel system of fiscal and financial governance are now on the table.[1] In this context, concepts such as tax harmonization, tax competition, and tax sovereignty are at the forefront of the debate on future EU fiscal policy.

Since the creation of modern nation-states, taxation has been a recurrent topic of discussion within the framework of intergovernmental relations, both in the domestic organization of states and at the international level—between states or within supranational organizations. Focusing on the domestic field, the distribution of the power of taxation is a key determinant in assessing the real and effective scope of the fiscal and financial power exercised by different institutions or levels of government.

As a result of the integration process over recent decades, the European Union has emerged as a new player in the European tax field. Even though the European central institutions *still do not have a direct role* in raising taxes or setting tax rates, their influence on taxation matters is

---

1 European Commission, *White Paper on the Future of Europe: Reflection and Scenarios for the EU27 by 2025* (Brussels: Publications Office of the European Union, 2017).

becoming increasingly determinant. In some regards, it is possible to draw parallels between the European integration process and certain liberal state-building processes that took place mainly during the nineteenth century. Just as the authority of liberal states was strengthened at the expense of sub-central "powers," the European Union is progressively concentrating more powers in its hands at the expense of the member states. There has been a role reversal: the member states are now acting as sub-central "powers," giving up sovereignty in favor of the European central institutions. In this regard, improving understanding of nation-state building processes can provide lessons for the ongoing process of European integration.

In accordance with these precedents, this chapter focuses on the exercise of tax power by Basque and Swiss sub-central governments, analyzing them from a historical perspective. On the one hand, Switzerland, by tradition, was and continues to be one of the most paradigmatic examples of European federalism. On the other, under the agreement system (Concierto Económico), the Basque provinces of Araba, Bizkaia, Gipuzkoa, and Navarre[2] formed an exception within the Kingdom of Spain, shaping a federal-type system of fiscal and financial relations between these provinces and the state. By comparing and contrasting the two case studies, the chapter aims to identify key factors involved in nation-state building processes in federal systems. In particular, the benchmarking exercise places special emphasis on the extent and impact of the institutional changes in the tax landscape. For that purpose, the article is structured in four sections.

The first section establishes the historical and institutional framework of both realities. The second and third sections analyze and compare the extent and scope of the fiscal and financial self-government exercised by Basque and Swiss sub-central governments in the first third of the twentieth century and from the last third of the twentieth century to the present. The final section provides some conclusions and reflections on the European integration process.

---

2 Navarre, under the Economic Covenant (Convenio Económico) was organized according to a system that was similar, though not identical, to that enjoyed in the Araba, Bizkaia, and Gipuzkoa, thanks to the Economic Agreement. On the evolution and confluence of the two systems from their creation until the outbreak of the Spanish Civil War in 1936, see Mikel Aranburu, "Evolución De Los Conciertos Y Convenios Económicos Hasta 1936. Una Perspectiva Comparada," *Iura Vasconiae* 10 (2013), 219–78.

HISTORICAL AND INSTITUTIONAL DEVELOPMENT OF THE BASQUE COUNTRY AND SWITZERLAND

The choice of Switzerland and the Basque Country as case studies is not a matter of chance. They provide empirical examples of the complexity and divisiveness emanating from intergovernmental relations regarding the distribution of powers and responsibilities among models of fiscal federalism.

Until the nineteenth century, Switzerland had been structured as a confederal state, in which the central state, the Confederation, played a subsidiary role. Under the *foral* system, the Basque provinces of Araba, Bizkaia, Gipuzkoa, and Navarre each enjoyed extremely broad self-government, operating *de facto* like a "*sui generis* confederation."[3] The nineteenth century marked a watershed in the configuration of the *res publica* in both cases. The liberal revolution that traversed Europe during the nineteenth century, together with other factors of change like industrialization, completely transformed their structures of government and administrative organization.

In the nineteenth century, abandoning its confederal tradition, Switzerland was consolidated as a federal state. In the context of the Liberal Revolution and after a brief civil war in 1847, the liberals imposed their state project with the approval of the "Federal Constitution of the Swiss Confederation" in 1848.[4] Although the title of the new Constitution maintained the denomination "Confederation of Switzerland," the Constitution of 1848 laid the foundations of a federal state. Drawing inspiration from the US Constitution, a National Council and Council of States were created, and a Federal Court was instituted. Additionally, the unification of customs, money and weights, and measures was established. The Confederation was exclusively empowered to coin money and was equipped with its own revenues proceeding from its management of customs rights.[5]

---

3   José Antonio de Aguirre y Lekube, "Prólogo," in *País Vasco y Estado Español. La solución Argentina* (Buenos Aires: Ekin, 1951).
4   Paolo Dardanelli, "El federalismo suizo: Orígenes, evolución y desafíos," in *Sistemas federales. Una comparación internacional* (Madrid: Konrad Adenauer Atiftung–Fundación Manuel Giménez Abad, 2017), 233–34.
5   Oswald Sigg, *Las Instituciones Políticas En Suiza* (Zürich: Pro Helvetia, 1988).

From the approval of the Federal Constitution in 1848 until World War II, a gradual process of centralization developed in favor of the Confederation and to the detriment of cantonal power. Facing the extraordinary situation arising from the two world wars, the Confederation strengthened and expanded its tax power. Following World War II and in a context of bitter debates between those positions that demanded greater centralization and the defenders of maintaining the widest possible cantonal autonomy, a review process took place, consolidating large parts of the "extraordinary and provisional" reforms implemented during the wartime periods.

After various decades without any significant alterations, a new Constitution was approved in 1999, which updated the previous one of 1848.[6] In comparison with other European countries, Switzerland has enjoyed a high degree of political and institutional continuity from the beginning of the twentieth century up to the present day. Among other questions, the institutional map has not suffered structural changes throughout this period. The administrative structure has remained divided into three main levels: the Confederation, the cantons, and the municipalities. It should be recalled that as a consequence of a negative vote in the referendum in 1992, Switzerland decided not to form part of the EU.

The process of deep transformations undergone by the Basque Country in the nineteenth century had certain parallels with what has been described for the Swiss case. Prior to the construction of the liberal Spanish state, a process that developed over the course of the nineteenth century, the Kingdom of Spain was articulated as a composite monarchy in which other alternative powers coexisted alongside the central administration,[7] including the Basque representative institutions.

Under the foral system the Basque provinces enjoyed extremely broad self-government. Joseba Agirreazkuenaga defines the *fueros* as "a series of laws, customs, privileges, liberties, exemptions, that formed the basic rules of social, economic, juridical, legal and political life according to General Assemblies for inhabitants of the Basque Country, guaranteeing a significant level of self-rule and self-government."[8] Although its origin

---

6   Remedio Sánchez and María Vicenta García, *Suiza. Sistema político y constitución* (Madrid: Centro de Estudios políticos y constitucionales, 2002).
7   Joseba Agirreazkuenaga, *The Making of the Basque Question: Experiencing Self-Government, 1793–1877* (Reno: Center for Basque Studies, University of Nevada, Reno, 2011).
8   Ibid., 256–57.

dates back to the Middle Ages, under the liberal conception of the nineteenth century the foral system could be compared to a constitutional system, in which each province had its own *"foral* constitution."[9]

In the context of the Liberal Revolution of the nineteenth century, the survival and strengthening of the peripheral powers of the Basque Country around the Basque representative institutions clashed with the process of building and expanding of the Spanish liberal state. Together with other factors, this state of competition between different powers was decisive in explaining the origin of the series of harsh civil wars that ravaged the Basque Country during the nineteenth century. Following the victory of the liberal troops in the final Carlist War (1872–1876), the state, in an act of centralist imposition, abolished the foral system *"manu militari"* and against the will of the Basque representative institutions.

Two years after the abolition of the foral system, the Basque and Spanish governments negotiated the Economic Agreement as the system by which the Basque provinces would contribute to the finances of the Kingdom of Spain.[10] The content and extent of the self-government emanating from the agreement system that began with the Royal Decree of February 28, 1878 bore little resemblance to the prior situation. Extensive self-government was reduced to economic-administrative autonomy. In the fiscal and financial fields, the Basque provinces continued to exercise a broad self-government. But in other spheres, such as political-institutional organization, the administration of justice, and military questions, the provinces were fully integrated into the common and uniform framework of the state.

At the end of the nineteenth and beginning of the twentieth century, the Economic Agreement was consolidated as the instrument regulating taxation and financial relations between the Basque and Spanish central administrations. But the outbreak of the Civil War in 1936 altered the situation dramatically. Following the capture of Bilbao by the rebel troops in June 1937, the Economic Agreement was abolished in Bizkaia and Gipuzkoa. The new dictatorial regime described the provinces of Bizkaia and Gipuzkoa as "traitors" because of their support for the republican

---

9   Joseba Agirreazkuenaga, "Resilience of Foral Tax Systems During the Liberal Revolution (1793–1937)," in *The Basque Fiscal System: History, Current Status and Future Perspectives,* ed. Joseba Agirreazkuenaga and Eduardo Alonso (Reno: Center for Basque Studies, University of Nevada, Reno, 2014).

10   Eduardo J. Alonso, *El Concierto Económico (1878–1937). Orígenes y formación de un derecho histórico* (Oñate: IVAP, 1995). On the history of the Economic Agreement, see also, http://www.conciertoeconomico.org/en/.

legality of the time, in this way justifying its decision to eliminate the Economic Agreement in both provinces. Conversely, the Economic Agreement and Covenant continued in force respectively in Araba and Navarre throughout the entire Franco period.

Not only did the abolition of the Economic Agreement in Bizkaia and Gipuzkoa mark the end of a stage in the vital life of the agreement system, but it also was a milestone in the gradual process of centralization and homogenization that, since the nineteenth century, had been gradually subjecting and subordinating the self-government power of the Basque representative institutions in favor of the central institutions of the unitary Spanish state.

More than forty years had to pass until, following the death of the dictator Francisco Franco in 1975, an intricate process of negotiation with the state started that culminated in the recovery and updating of Basque self-government, based on the 1978 Spanish Constitution, the 1979 Autonomy Statute, and the 1981 Economic Agreement Law. The 1979 Autonomy Statute, currently in force, establishes the Autonomous Community of the Basque Country that encompasses the provinces of Araba, Bizkaia, and Gipuzkoa. The statute also reinstituted the Basque government as a supra-provincial authority, situated between the state and the provinces. Furthermore, after Spain's entry into the European Economic Community in 1986—today part of the European Union—the European institutions came onto the institutional scene. The Basque institutional landscape has undergone a deep transformation over the last century. While three levels of administration—state, provinces and municipalities—coexisted for most of the twentieth century, following the incorporation of the Basque government and European institutions, it now consists of five levels.

Before concluding this historical and institutional contextualization, we should underscore one key characteristic that is concurrent in the two cases: the procedure for assigning powers between central and sub-central governments has not been the result of a process of decentralization. [11] The construction of the Swiss federal state is a clear example of a "bottom-up construction" process. It has been the cantons, formed in their turn by municipalities, that gradually and in response to circumstances have transferred power and competencies to the Confederation and not the reverse. It can thus be understood that up until today, originary

---

11   Adrian Vatter, "Federalism," in *Handbook of Swiss Politics* (Zürich: Neue Zürcher Zeitung Publishing, 2007).

sovereignty and residual powers have remained in the hands of the cantons, not of central power.[12]

Although the Basque case is somewhat problematic, the logic of the transfer of powers between administrations follows the same pattern. Irrespective of possible legal interpretations of the formal link that might exist between the foral system and the agreement system, in terms of government practice what took place in the Basque Country was not a process of decentralization but of concentration. When the state abolished the foral system it absorbed part of the functions that until then had depended on the foral governments. But in those areas of the public function that—on occasions by *de iure* means and on others by *de facto* ones—remained under the authority of the Basque administrations, there was no effective process for the devolution of powers given that they had not previously been centralized. For example, in Araba and Navarre, where the fiscal and financial self-government system survived during the Franco's dictatorship, the state, from the foral period to the present, has never developed the bulk of the rail network or carried out forestry management, nor has it managed or collected the main direct taxes.

THE TAX POWER OF THE BASQUE AND SWISS SUB-CENTRAL GOVERNMENTS IN THE FIRST THIRD OF THE TWENTIETH CENTURY

Restricting ourselves to the fiscal and financial domain, the Swiss federal system and the Basque agreement system bore reasonable similarities with respect to their organization, extent, and functioning. In both cases, the distribution of tax powers and responsibilities was divided into three main level of government: the central state, called the Confederation in Switzerland; the Swiss cantons or Basque provinces as sub-central governments; and the municipalities.[13]

The cantonal and provincial governments exercised extensive tax power and had broad financial autonomy. In both systems, the framework

---

12   Sánchez and García, *Suiza*, 81.
13   This section is summarized from Mikel Erkoreka, "The Public Finances of Araba, Bizkaia and Gipuzkoa during the Dictatorship, the Great Depression and the II Republic (1925–1937): A Comparative Analysis with Switzerland and a Contribution to Fiscal Federalism Theory," PhD diss., University of the Basque Country, 2017, 249–97.

of fiscal relations between administrations was articulated on two levels: between the central state and the sub-central entities on the one hand, and within the framework of the sub-central entities—sub-central governments and municipalities—on the other. Among other questions, the control of municipal treasuries and the design of the municipal financing systems corresponded in both cases to sub-central governments and not to the central government. Therefore, each sub-central entity had its own system of municipal financing.

In general terms, the dispersal of fiscal powers between the sub-central and central tax authorities followed a logic based on the nature of the taxes: direct taxes were under the control of the sub-central governments while the state controlled indirect taxes.

Due to the broad freedom of fiscal self-government that sub-central governments enjoyed in both the Basque Country and Switzerland, there were clear differences between the domestic tax systems. For example, not all the sub-central tax authorities collected the same taxes. With respect to the taxes they decided to levy, each authority, without harmonizing restrictions, decided on the substantial elements of the different taxes, such as tax bases, tax rates, and tax allowances. The same happened with the work of collection, settlement, and inspection. Among other questions, the distribution of the function of tax collection between the sub-central and municipal administrations was decided at the cantonal or provincial level.

In the case of Switzerland, each canton had its own tax administration, which when added to that of the Confederation resulted in twenty-six different tax authorities in a territory with slightly over four million inhabitants. Meanwhile, regarding the Basque Country, five tax authorities coexisted within the Spanish Kingdom prior to the Civil War, which broke out in 1936: the state tax administration and one for each Basque province of Araba, Bizkaia, Gipuzkoa, and Navarre.

The coexistence of multiple fiscal governments with very wide faculties of action provided a favorable platform for inter-territorial tax competition. Tax competition was a widespread and common practice in Switzerland, at both the cantonal and municipal levels. For example, there were great differences in the tax rates applied between cantons. But tax rates were not the only element to bear in mind. The use of other competitive instruments, such as whether or not to apply certain taxes, fiscal regulations referring to the sums exempted and deductions, or even the degree of scrupulousness in the work of inspection and collection, were all influential.[14]

As with the cantons, the Basque administrations were not subjected to harmonizing restrictions that might have significantly conditioned the exercise of their fiscal self-government. In this context, the Spanish tax administration repeatedly accused the Basque tax authorities of applying lower fiscal pressure on direct taxation and of practicing unfair tax competition. This situation generated strong suspicions in both Spanish public opinion and in the Spanish Treasury Department. Additionally, there were also cases of tax competition among the Basque provinces themselves.[15]

THE TAX POWER OF THE BASQUE AND SWISS SUB-CENTRAL GOVERNMENTS DURING THE LAST THIRD OF THE TWENTIETH CENTURY UP TO THE PRESENT

Obviously enough, in the course of nearly a century, Swiss and Basque fiscal system have undergone profound changes. However, the extent and intensity of the transformations differ considerably between both realities. In this regard, the development of the institutional setting is fundamental to understanding the evolution of the taxation powers of Basque and Swiss sub-central governments.

As pointed out above, Switzerland has experienced a high degree of institutional continuity since the beginning of the twentieth century. The Swiss administrative structure continues nowadays to be based on the same three levels of government: the Confederation, the cantons, and the municipalities. Concerning the distribution of tax powers, new relevant players, such as supra-cantonal entities or the European institutions, have not come onto the scene.[16]

The cantons continue to be empowered to levy any kind of tax provided that does not fall under the exclusive authority of the Confederation. Among others, the Confederation claims exclusive taxation authority in

---

14 Sébastien Güex, *L'Argent de l'etat. Parcours des finances publiques au XXe siècle* (Lausanne: Réalités sociales, 1998).

15 Eduardo J. Alonso, "La fiscalidad empresarial en Vizcaya 1914–1935. Un beneficio del Concierto Económico," *Hacienda Pública Española* 2–3 (1997), 3–26.

16 Ulrich Klöti, ed. *Handbook of Swiss Politics* (Zürich: Neue Zürcher Zeitung Publishing, 2007).

VAT (value added tax), special excise duties, stamp duties, withholding tax, and customs duties. In short, the traditional principle of separation, by which the Confederation managed and collected the indirect taxes and the cantons the direct ones, continues to guide the Swiss tax system. The cantons continue playing a prominent role regarding direct taxation, while the Confederation does so regarding indirect taxation. Consequently, the twenty-six cantons are given wide latitude in the creation of their own tax legislation.[17]

In the 1990s, the Federal Parliament approved and implemented the Federal Act on the Harmonization of Direct Taxation at Cantonal and Communal Levels. This is a framework law designed to harmonize certain formal aspects of cantonal direct taxation. But as the law, reflected in article 129 of the Federal Constitution of the Swiss Confederation, states, "harmonization shall [only] extend to tax liability, the object of the tax and the tax period, procedural law and law relating to tax offences. Matters excluded from harmonization shall include in particular tax scales, tax rates and tax allowances."

Any attempt to make significant progress on the path of tax harmonization over and above the formal aspects has failed in Switzerland. The popular initiative "For fair taxation. Stop abuses of tax competition" (*Pour des impôts* équitables. *Stop aux abus de la concurrence fiscal*) illustrates this. This initiative, launched by the Socialist Party, was intended to limit tax competition and introduce a minimum cantonal tax rate for high incomes. But the initiative submitted to a referendum in 2010 was rejected at both the federal and cantonal levels.

In this way, the cantons continue operating today in a poorly harmonized framework, in which inter-cantonal tax competition is still a widespread practice.[18] Consequently, there are significant differences in the tax pressure within Switzerland, not only among cantons, but also from one municipality to another within the same canton. As in the early twentieth century, not all cantons collected the same taxes. With respect to the taxes they decided to levy, each authority decided on the substantial elements of the different taxes, such as tax scales, tax rates,

---

17   Federal Tax Administration, *The Swiss Tax System* (Bern: Swiss Tax Conference Information Committee, 2017); Federal Department of Finance, *Federal, Cantonal and Communal Taxes* (Bern: Swiss Confederation, 2016).

18   Mikel Erkoreka, "El Federalismo fiscal suizo desde la perspectiva del País Vasco," in *Federalismo fiscal y concierto económico. Una aproximación desde el derecho comparado* (Vitoria-Gasteiz: Eusko Legebiltzarra-Parlamento Vasco, 2016), 59–64.

and tax allowances. The same happened with the work of collection, settlement, and inspection.

In contrast to Switzerland, the Basque fiscal and financial system has undergone deeper transformations. In the late 1970s, following the death of Franco, Basque representatives negotiated a new Economic Agreement with the Spanish government, approved by law in 1981.[19] In this way, the agreement system was updated and recovered in Bizkaia and Gipuzkoa, once again encompassing the three provinces. The Economic Covenant of Navarre was subsequently revised.

The adoption of the 1978 Spanish Constitution, the 1979 Autonomy Statute, and the 1981 Economic Agreement Law completely changed Basque fiscal, financial, political, and institutional organization. Under the Autonomy Statute a new administrative entity was established: the Autonomous Community of the Basque Country (ACBC), which encompasses the Historical Territories, or provinces, of Araba, Bizkaia, and Gipuzkoa. Navarre was articulated as a single-province autonomous community. Soon after, in 1986, Spain joined the European Economic Community, adopting common European rules and standards.[20]

Consequently, the institutional setting of the ACBC is currently structured on five levels of government: the European Union; the state; the Basque government; the provincial governments of the Historical Territories of Araba, Bizkaia, and Gipuzkoa; and the municipalities.

Moving from the institutional to the fiscal area, the 1981 Economic Agreement Law regulates the taxation and financial relations between the Spanish tax administration and the ACBC. The Economic Agreement Law acknowledges that institutions of the Historical Territories of Araba, Bizkaia, and Gipuzkoa "may maintain, establish and regulate, within their territory, their taxation system." In addition, it added that, "the levying, administration, settlement, inspection, revision and collection of the taxes and duties comprising the taxation system of the Historical Territories shall be the responsibility of the respective territorial governments."[21]

---

19   Pedro Luis Uriarte, "The Economic Agreement of 1981," in *The Basque Fiscal System: History, Current Status and Future Perspectives*, ed. Joseba Agirreazkuenaga and Eduardo Alonso (Reno: Center for Basque Studies, University of Nevada, Reno, 2014).

20   On the political, institutional and fiscal organization of the ACBC, see Ignacio Zubiri, *The Economic Agreement between the Basque Country and Spain: Principles, Characteristics and Economic Implications* (Bilbao: Ad Concordiam, 2010), 38–48.

21   Organ of Tributary Coordination of Basque Country, *Economic Agreement* (Vitoria-Gasteiz: Publications Office of the Basque Government, 2009), 245.

In this way, the Basque provincial governments continue empowered to exercise an extensive fiscal and financial self-government. They are among the sub-state authorities in Europe that have the most tax power. But even so, compared to the previous period, the fiscal autonomy and normative capacity of the Basque tax authorities are subjected to stricter limitations today. These constraints arise mainly from the multilevel tax harmonization powers. In particular, the Basque tax authorities are subjected to a "triple tax harmonization" fostered and implemented by the European institutions, the state, and the Basque parliament.[22] In the words of Gemma Martínez, "the Basque Country region is a rare bird among regions with wide taxation powers; no other region in the federal system is involved in so many tax harmonization levels."[23]

Starting from the first field of tax harmonization, the European Union *does not have a direct role* in raising taxes or setting tax rates. Tax legislation is mainly decided by each country of the European Union at the national level. But in order to ensure that competition in the single market is not distorted, the European Commission can present proposals for tax legislation. It can also make recommendations and issue policy guidance in specific areas. All the EU members must unanimously agree on any EU tax legislation. Within this framework, the European Union has implemented measures to coordinate and harmonize indirect taxes such as value added tax (VAT) and excise duties. Separately, the harmonization of direct taxation has been minimal to date.[24]

At the domestic level, the Economic Agreement Law establishes several general principles regarding the harmonization of Basque tax legislations with that of the state. Among other questions, the Basque fiscal systems shall "respect the state tax law in matters of terminology and concepts" and "maintain an overall effective fiscal pressure equivalent to that in force in the rest of the State."[25] Although it may seem paradoxical, the

---

22 Gemma Martínez, *Armonización fiscal y poder tributario foral en la Comunidad Autónoma del País Vasco* (Oñati: IVAP, 2014).
23 Gemma Martínez, "Tax Harmonization in Federal Systems: The Basque Case," in *The Basque Fiscal System Contrasted to Nevada and Catalonia in the Time of Major Crises*, ed. Joseba Agirreazkuenaga and Xabier Irujo (Reno: Center for Basque Studies, University of Nevada, Reno, 2016), 153.
24 European Parliament, *Tax Policy in the EU. Issues and Challenges* (European Parliamentary Research Service, 2015); European Commission, *The European Union Explained: Taxation* (Luxembourg: Publications Office of the European Union, 2015); Gemma Martínez, "Armonización fiscal y capacidad normativa de los territorios históricos del País Vasco (I)," *Zergak: gaceta tributaria del País Vasco* 43 (2012), 65–78.
25 Organ of Tributary Coordination of Basque Country, *Economic Agreement*, 246.

current decentralized Spanish state model establishes more harmonizing restrictions on Basque fiscal self-government than was the case under the previous unitary state models of both Restoration and Francoist Spain.

Finally, the internal tax harmonization among the Historical Territories has to be taken into consideration. The ACBC is organized internally as a federal or even confederal fiscal system.

As has been noted above, under the agreement system the bulk of tax powers remain in the hands of provincial or sub-central tax authorities. The Basque parliament and government—acting within the ACBC as central administration—enjoyed limited tax power with respect to the three Basque provinces. The Autonomy Statute and Economic Agreement Law allow the Basque parliament to promote the "coordination, fiscal harmonization and mutual cooperation between the Historical Territories institutions." To that end, in 1989 the Basque parliament adopted the Tax Harmonization Law, which "allowed the Basque Parliament to eliminate, if necessary, essential differences among the tax systems of the Historical Territories," for example, in tax rates or the tax treatment of certain items.[26] Thanks to the Harmonization Law, the Basque Tax Coordination Committee was created, whose function is to promote fiscal harmonization, cooperation, and coordination among the tax administrations of Araba, Bizkaia, and Gipuzkoa.[27]

The Basque government is almost entirely financed on the basis of provincial governments' financial transfers. After collecting the taxes, the sub-central governments of Araba, Bizkaia, and Gipuzkoa transfer most of their revenues to the Basque government (around 70 percent). Therefore, despite the limited taxation power exercised by the Basque government, after the transfer, it enjoys a higher effective expenditure capacity than the provincial and municipal governments.

In this respect there are certain parallels between the ACBC and EU multilevel fiscal and financial governance systems. As explained above, EU intervention in taxation matters has mostly been confined to harmonizing indirect taxation. The financial transfers of member states are the largest source of income of the EU budget, accounting for around 70 to 80 percent of the revenue side. In contrast with the Basque government budget, the EU expenditure budget stands out due to its

---

26 Zubiri, *The Economic Agreement between the Basque Country and Spain*, 59–60.
27 Gemma Martínez, "Armonización fiscal y capacidad normativa de los territorios históricos del País Vasco (III)," *Zergak: gaceta tributaria del País Vasco*, no. 45 (2013), 73–90.

relatively small size and lack of flexibility. The EU budget, in accordance with the Treaties, cannot exceed 1.23 percent of the aggregate Gross National Income of the member states, nor can it close with a deficit.[28]

To conclude the Basque case analysis, the "triple harmonization" that nowadays affects the Basque tax authorities significantly limits their fiscal autonomy and normative capacity. In comparison with the Swiss case, among other issues, the Basque tax authorities now have much less room for fiscal competency.

CONCLUSIONS AND REFLECTIONS ON THE EUROPEAN INTEGRATION PROCESS

As in the nation-state building processes, any kind of in-depth integration process requires a long-term perspective. The current state of the Basque and Swiss tax systems is the end of a long process of successes and failures, as well as the result of intricate processes of intergovernmental conflicts and negotiations. In this context, the European Union is still a very recently created organization. In areas such as monetary union, which in many countries has been achieved after a lengthy process of maturation, the European Union has taken a quantum leap forward in a few decades. The current juncture characterized by large adverse shocks—for instance the economic crisis or the political and institutional challenge caused by the Brexit—must be viewed from this long-term perspective. Most of today's European states have overcome much more serious internal crises during the process of their construction. In this sense, situations of turmoil such as the current one should not be seen as only posing a risk, but also as an opportunity for consolidating the rapid progress made so far and for reflecting on the future of the European Union.

The institutional changes are fundamental for understanding the divergent evolution of the taxation powers of Basque and Swiss sub-central governments from the early twentieth century up to the present. In comparison with the Swiss case, the Basque tax landscape has been profoundly affected by the emergence of new relevant players such as

---

28   John McCormick, *Understanding the European Union: A Concise Introduction* (London: Palgrave, 2017).

the European Union or the Basque autonomous institutions. In that context, any future reform in the institutional setting will have to be studied very carefully.

The emergence of a new "competency" requires reformulating and reconfiguring the assigning of tax power and responsibilities, with all the political and technical challenges that this involves. The distribution of taxation power is a key determinant for calibrating the real and effective scope of the power that is assigned to each institution or level of government. Tax power has been and continues to be the central axis around which Basque and Swiss sub-central institutions self-government pivot. Aware of this, Basque and Swiss sub-central institutions have shown great resiliency and resistance in order to preserve as much taxation power as possible under their authority.

The European integration process is following a similar pattern. The attempts to move forward the fiscal integration faced the reluctance of the member states to cede any tax sovereignty. But still, if the European institutions want to increase their capacity of intervention on the European economy—see, for instance, the cohesion policies or the fiscal stabilization function—its fiscal and financial power should be strengthened in order to provide more funds to the still meager EU budget. The Swiss and Basque cases show two possible alternatives: claiming direct taxation powers over some taxes, such as certain indirect taxes; or increasing the amount of the sub-central governments' financial transfers. Any changes in this respect will largely determine the fiscal path that the European Union takes between federalization and a more confederal type of system.

BIBLIOGRAPHY

Agirreazkuenaga, Joseba. *The Making of the Basque Question: Experiencing Self-Government, 1793–1877.* Reno: Center for Basque Studies, University of Nevada, Reno, 2011.

———. "Resilience of Foral Tax Systems During the Liberal Revolution (1793–1937)." In *The Basque Fiscal System: History, Current Status and Future Perspectives,* edited by Joseba Agirreazkuenaga and Eduardo Alonso. Reno: Center for Basque Studies, University of Nevada, Reno, 2014.

Aguirre y Lekube, José Antonio de. "Prólogo." In *País Vasco y Estado Español. La Solución Argentina*. Buenos Aires: Ekin, 1951.

Alonso, Eduardo J. *El Concierto Económico (1878–1937). Orígenes y formación de un derecho histórico*. Oñate: IVAP, 1995.

———. "La fiscalidad empresarial en Vizcaya 1914–1935. Un beneficio del concierto económico." *Hacienda Pública Española* 2–3 (1997): 3–26.

Aranburu, Mikel. "Evolución de los conciertos y convenios económicos hasta 1936. Una perspectiva comparada." *Iura Vasconiae* 10 (2013): 219–78.

Dardanelli, Paolo. "El federalismo suizo: orígenes, evolución y desafíos." In *Sistemas federales. Una comparación internacional*. Madrid: Konrad Adenauer Atiftung–Fundación Manuel Giménez Abad, 2017.

Erkoreka, Mikel. "El Federalismo fiscal suizo desde la perspectiva del País Vasco." In *Federalismo fiscal y Concierto Económico. Una aproximación desde el derecho comparado*. Vitoria-Gasteiz: Eusko Legebiltzarra-Parlamento Vasco, 2016.

———. "The Public Finances of Araba, Bizkaia and Gipuzkoa During the Dictatorship, the Great Depression and the II Republic (1925–1937): A Comparative Analysis with Switzerland and a Contribution to Fiscal Federalism Theory." PhD Dissertation, University of the Basque Country, 2017.

European Commision. *The European Union Explained: Taxation*. Luxembourg: Publications Office of the European Union, 2015.

———. *White Paper on the Future of Europe: Reflection and Scenarios for the EU27 by 2025*. Brussels: Publications Office of the European Union, 2017.

European Parliament. *Tax Policy in the EU: Issues and Challenges*. European Parliamentary Research Service, 2015.

Federal Department of Finance. *Federal, Cantonal and Communal Taxes*. Bern: Swiss Confederation, 2016.

Federal Tax Administration. *The Swiss Tax System*. Bern: Swiss Tax Conference Information Committee, 2017.

Güex, Sébastien. *L´Argent de l´etat. Parcours des finances publiques au XXe siècle*. Lausanne: Réalités sociales, 1998.

Klöti, Ulrich, ed. *Handbook of Swiss Politics*. Zürich: Neue Zürcher Zeitung Publishing, 2007.

Martínez Barbara, Gemma. "Armonización fiscal y capacidad normativa de los territorios históricos del País Vasco (I)." *Zergak: gaceta tributaria del País Vasco* 43 (2012): 65–78.

———. "Armonización fiscal y capacidad normativa de los territorios históricos del País Vasco (III)." *Zergak: gaceta tributaria del País Vasco* 45 (2013): 73–90.

———. *Armonización fiscal y poder tributario foral en la comunidad autónoma del País Vasco*. Oñati: IVAP, 2014.

———. "Tax Harmonization in Federal Systems: The Basque Case." In *The Basque Fiscal System Contrasted to Nevada and Catalonia in the Time of Major Crises*, edited by Joseba Agirreazkuenaga and Xabier Irujo. Reno: Center for Basque Studies, University of Nevada, Reno, 2016.

McCormick, John. *Understanding the European Union: A Concise Introduction*. London: Palgrave, 2017.

Organ of Tributary Coordination of Basque Country. *Economic Agreement*. Vitoria-Gasteiz: Publications Office of the Basque Government, 2009.

Sánchez, Remedio, and María Vicenta García. *Suiza. Sistema político y Constitución*. Madrid: Centro de Estudios políticos y constitucionales, 2002.

Sigg, Oswald. *Las Instituciones Políticas En Suiza*. Zürich: Pro Helvetia, 1988.

Uriarte, Pedro Luis. "The Economic Agreement of 1981." In *The Basque Fiscal System: History, Current Status and Future Perspectives*, edited by Joseba Agirreazkuenga and Eduardo Alonso. Reno: Center for Basque Studies, University of Nevada, Reno, 2014.

Vatter, Adrian. "Federalism." In *Handbook of Swiss Politics*. Zürich: Neue Zürcher Zeitung Publishing, 2007.

Zubiri, Ignacio. *The Economic Agreement between the Basque Country and Spain: Principles, Characteristics and Economic Implications*. Bilbao: Ad Concordiam, 2010.

Chapter 6

A Fiscal Model for Political Cosovereignty? How the Economic Agreement Has Shaped the Territorial Ambitions of Basque Nationalists

Caroline Gray

Traditionally, it is the Basques who have shown more inclination to seek sovereignty and fundamental constitutional change than the Catalans. Not surprisingly, it was the Basque nationalists who first devised a pro-sovereignty agenda. This took the form of the revised autonomy statute proposal since known as the Ibarretxe Plan (named after the Basque regional president at the time, Juan José Ibarretxe), which was approved (albeit only just) by the Basque parliament in 2004 before being rejected by the Spanish parliament. Although the plan did not propose full independence, it envisaged fundamental changes to Spain's constitutional order by proposing to redefine the Basque relationship with Spain as one of free association, thus opening the door to a self-determination referendum.[1] The traditionally mainstream Catalan nationalist party, then named Democratic Convergence of Catalonia (Convergència Democràtica de Catalunya, CDC), did not explicitly shift toward a pro-sovereignty agenda until several years later, in 2012, following tentative developments in this direction from around 2008. Why is it, then, that the thwarting of Ibarretxe's proposals ultimately resulted in the Basque Nationalist Party (Partido Nacionalista Vasco,

---

1   Michael Keating and Zoe Bray, "Renegotiating Sovereignty: Basque Nationalism and the Rise and Fall of the Ibarretxe Plan," *Ethnopolitics* 5, no. 4 (2006): 347–64.

PNV) de-emphasizing its territorial ambitions under the leadership of Iñigo Urkullu, whereas pro-independence politicians in Catalonia decided to defy Madrid and push ahead with their plans regardless?

Several contributing factors to these differences can be identified, not least the fact that there has been much higher civil society mobilization for independence in Catalonia in recent years, whereas the Ibarretxe Plan was a heavily party-led initiative arguably lacking sufficient backing from society, as recognized by many within the PNV itself, both at the time and in hindsight.[2] These different levels of social mobilization can, in turn, be explained by factors including the recent history of terrorism in the Basque Country but not in Catalonia, and also the different levels of fiscal devolution in the two regions. Even if there is relatively limited knowledge and understanding among Basque society about how exactly the Basque Economic Agreement (*Concierto Económico*) works, citizens inevitably feel the benefits of higher public spending, since the model affords the Basque government much higher resources per capita than other regions under the common financing system receive. For many PNV politicians too, the positives of the Economic Agreement reduce the urgency to seek a new fit for the Basque Country within or with Spain. Moreover, the PNV has been concerned first and foremost in recent years with the impact of the global financial crisis of 2008 on the Basque region, which it has been the sole responsibility of the Basque government to address, since the fiscal autonomy model means it cannot shift blame onto the Spanish government for the region's financial woes, in contrast to the situation in Catalonia.

Nevertheless, the de-emphasizing of territorial politics under Iñigo Urkullu, PNV leader from 2009 and Basque regional president from 2012, did not mean the PNV had renounced its territorial objective of seeking a form of sovereignty for the Basque region. The party has remained committed to seeking a new status that would allow for bilateral relations between the Basque and Spanish governments as equal partners, including the right to Basque self-determination and cosovereignty with Spain. Under regional president Urkullu and party leader Andoni

2   The views of different political parties reflected in this chapter are informed primarily by an extensive program of personal interviews with current and former politicians that I conducted throughout a nine-month period of fieldwork in the Basque Country in 2014 as part of my doctoral research, funded by the Economic and Social Research Council (ESRC) of the UK [ES/J500094/1]. This chapter draws on some of the findings of my research, published as *Nationalist Politics and Regional Financing Systems in the Basque Country and Catalonia* (Bilbao: Foral Treasury Doctoral Thesis Collection, 2016).

Ortuzar (in the PNV, the regional president and party leader are two different roles), the PNV's conception of the cosovereignty it seeks has envisaged an extension of the bilateral nature of the Economic Agreement, whereby Spanish and Basque delegations have equal negotiating rights and veto power, to wider political relations. To this end, the PNV has made explicit calls in recent years for an equivalent bilateral Political Agreement, specifically named a "Concierto Político."[3] This chapter aims to analyze the PNV's vision and ambition in this regard, and the obstacles it faces to achieving it, for this is an important issue that has been somewhat overlooked amid heightened political and academic attention to the situation in Catalonia.

Before proceeding to the analysis, some terms in this chapter need to be clarified, particularly the word "sovereignty" as used in both fiscal and political contexts. In brief, fiscal *autonomy* when applied to substate governments usually describes a large degree of freedom in raising and spending taxes but still within the boundaries of some rules set by the wider state, following a process of fiscal decentralization. Fiscal *sovereignty*, meanwhile, is more often applied to states themselves and suggests complete autonomy in setting fiscal policies without any outside interference. In practice, complete fiscal sovereignty has now become almost obsolete in Europe since individual member states are subject to some wider European fiscal legislation, and the concept of sovereignty in general is increasingly problematic at a time of increasing European and global integration in many spheres. Here, however, fiscal sovereignty, when applied to the Basque provinces, describes the aspiration to reach the same level of sovereignty in setting tax structures and policies in most respects as held by Spain itself. Many representatives of the Basque institutions refer to the provinces as fiscally sovereign already in the case of taxes for which they have been granted regulatory autonomy, though this designation is not universally accepted by some statewide parties who consider the system one of fiscal decentralization rather than sovereignty, as discussed later in this chapter.

3　For example, "Ortuzar afirma que el PNV 'peleará mucho' por un Concierto politico que suponga cosoberanía," *Europa Press*, March 1, 2018. The standardized translation for the *"Concierto Económico"* is "Economic Agreement," but the general word "Agreement" inevitably loses the specific connotations of the word "Concierto," which has no direct translation in this context since there is no equivalent model in English. I have chosen to translate "Concierto Político" as "bilateral Political Agreement" in order to emphasize the allusions to bilateralism inherent in the term.

More broadly, when talking of wider political relations, pro-sovereignty politics involves a determined push by Basque and Catalan nationalists for their respective territories to be granted the "right to decide" their own political future and to be invested with sovereign political power, rather than this being the sole preserve of the Spanish state. It refers to their desire either for substantial changes to the Spanish legal and constitutional framework, or to break with it, in order to secure a fundamental reconfiguration of their respective territories' fit within or with Spain. Pro-sovereignty politics can, but does not have to, imply a push for full independence or secession. It can also imply attempts to reconstruct center-periphery relations on a different basis from the existing state of autonomies, involving a push for some form of confederalism involving bilateral relations and cosovereignty with the Spanish state.[4] Thus, pro-sovereignty politics includes Ibarretxe's thwarted attempt to upgrade the status of the Basque region to that of a semi-independent associated state of Spain, as well as the PNV's reconceptualization of this under Urkullu's leadership to envisage a bilateral Political Agreement.

The question of whether, and if so in what ways, increased fiscal devolution in the Basque Country has interacted with other drivers to reduce regional demands for independence is an important one, at a time when it is often assumed that fiscal devolution will help to accommodate nationalist movements seeking sovereignty. In the Scottish case, for example, much of the debate on strengthening the Scottish parliament within the United Kingdom, both in the lead-up to the 2014 independence referendum and in the wake of the no vote, centered on options for further fiscal devolution beyond the relatively limited fiscal powers afforded under the Scotland Act 2012. Further fiscal devolution subsequently began to be implemented in 2016. In the Catalan case, the Spanish government's refusal to devolve further fiscal powers under a "fiscal pact" akin to the Basque model undoubtedly contributed to the rise of pro-sovereignty sentiment, including the CDC's shift away from accommodationism and toward a pro-independence agenda.[5] Ultimately, however, this was overtaken by the broader clash between the Spanish government and Catalan pro-independence forces that is not solely or primarily economic in nature.

4   Richard Gillespie, "Between Accommodation and Contestation: The Political Evolution of Basque and Catalan Nationalism," *Nationalism and Ethnic Politics* 21, no. 1 (2015), 10.

5   Gray, *Nationalist Politics and Regional Financing Systems*, 201–41.

This chapter suggests that there is a relationship between increased fiscal devolution and reduced secessionism in the Basque case to an extent, but that it is a complex relationship rather than a straightforward one. The level of fiscal authority that the Economic Agreement gives the Basque region, combined with the high level of resources per capita the model affords, reduces the PNV's urgency to seek a new fit for the Basque region within or with Spain. Nevertheless, the Economic Agreement has not actually lessened the PNV's ambition ultimately to achieve some degree of political sovereignty. Rather, it has provided a prototype for the kind of political sovereignty they seek.

THE PNV's VISION OF FISCAL AND POLITICAL COSOVEREIGNTY

Under the Economic Agreement, the Basque authorities collect and regulate almost all taxes in the Basque region within the parameters of harmonization rules with Spanish tax legislation. They keep most of these proceeds (usually around 90 percent) to pay for devolved policy competences and use the remainder to pay an annual "quota" (*cupo*) to the Spanish government to contribute to the few remaining centralized competences.[6] What interests us about the Economic Agreement here, however, is not just the level of fiscal authority it affords, but its bilateral nature, whereby both Spanish and Basque delegations have equal negotiating rights and veto power. The bilateral nature of the Economic Agreement has helped to mitigate the problem of inter-regional competition for resources that afflicts the common financing system, as well as the perceived dominance of the Spanish government's interests in wider Spanish-regional government relations. The Law on the Economic Agreement and other legislation deriving from it (fundamentally the five-yearly quota laws governing the Basque contribution to the Spanish state) require mutual agreement between Basque and Spanish government delegations, both of which have equal veto power. The legislation is then always presented to the Spanish parliament as a single act; thus, it can only be accepted or rejected, without being subject to extensive parliamentary debate and potential partial amendment.

Instances when substantial Spanish-Basque differences of opinion over how to develop the Economic Agreement have been resolved using

---

6   For more details, see Gray, *Nationalist Politics and Regional Financing Systems*, 99–106.

technical arguments first and foremost, without one side simply ceding ground to the other in light of other contextual or political factors, have been rare in the decades since the first Economic Agreement of the democratic period was approved in 1981. There are a select few examples where both sides have held a similar position on key questions from early on in negotiations, as in the case of the decision made by the People's Party (Partido Popular, PP)-led absolute majority Spanish government and the PNV-led Basque government to make the Economic Agreement a permanent rather than time-limited agreement for the first time under the 2002 law. For most major questions, however, strong differences between the Basque and Spanish delegations have made it impossible to find a common middle ground and thus prevented agreements until, if, and when Spanish minority governments have needed the PNV's support in the Spanish parliament on other matters, and have accepted the Basque delegation's proposals for the Economic Agreement in return, as part of a classic "mutual backscratching" arrangement.[7]

A significant recent example of this was in 2017, when the PNV supported the weak Spanish PP government's budget in return for the resolution of disagreements in relation to the Economic Agreement that had beset Spanish-Basque fiscal and financial relations for a decade. The quota is calculated according to five-yearly quota laws, under a complex (and often, disputed) methodology agreed upon bilaterally between the Basque and Spanish authorities, which takes into account factors such as the valuation of devolved competences. Prior to the collaboration over the budget, none of the quotas since 2007 had been settled due to continuing Basque-Spanish government discrepancies over the valuation of the quota, and therefore no agreement had been reached on a new quota law for the period from 2012 onward either (the 2007–2011 one had simply been rolled over). The details of the new quota law for 2017–2021, fleshed out in the draft legislation approved by both the Basque and Spanish sides on July 19, 2017, following the political collaboration over the budget in May, revealed that it was not just the numbers that had now been agreed. Further revenue-raising powers were also to be devolved to the Basques in areas where there was still scope to do so.[8]

---

7   Gray, *Nationalist Politics and Regional Financing Systems*, 125–43. On "mutual backscratching" in general, see Bonnie N. Field, "Minority Parliamentary Government and Multilevel Politics: Spain's System of Mutual Back Scratching," *Comparative Politics* 46, no. 3 (2014), 293–312.

8   Spanish government press release, "El Estado y el País Vasco acuerdan la nueva Ley de Cupo que aclara y aporta estabilidad a las relaciones financieras entre

The functioning of the bilateral mechanism inherent within the Economic Agreement is thus far from optimal, since agreements are hardly ever reached on technical criteria alone, but rather tend to remain pending until the central government needs the PNV's support on other issues. Nevertheless, the fact that both sides have veto power has prevented the Spanish side from being able to unilaterally impose its view of how to update the Economic Agreement legislation or settle the quota payments. In fiscal and financial matters pertaining to the Economic Agreement, the Spanish government cannot take action such as approving a basic law that supersedes regional competences, in contrast to what can happen in other areas. For the PNV, this bilateralism in fiscal and financial matters, which they conceive of as a relationship between equals, is sacrosanct and contrasts with what they see as a subordination of Basque interests to Madrid in wider politics. This makes the Economic Agreement the best model for the form of "bilateral relationship between equals" that the PNV seeks in wider Spanish-Basque political relations, under the party's latest iteration of its recurring desire to seek a new political relationship with Madrid based on a more confederal model involving self-determination and cosovereignty.

Explicit reference by senior PNV representatives to the notion of a bilateral Political Agreement started to be made publically around 2014.[9] By then, the PNV under Urkullu had been back in power at regional government level for a couple of years, after unexpectedly being pushed into opposition from 2009–2012 due to a highly unusual coalition government between the PP and the Basque Socialist Party (Partido Socialista de Euskadi, PSE, the Basque branch of the Spanish Socialist Party, Partido Socialista Obrero Español, PSOE). Also by then, Urkullu had also restored the PNV's traditional relationship with the Basque Socialists, which had been broken for over a decade when the parties in the Basque Country divided into nationalist and non-nationalist blocs starting with the Lizarra Pact, signed by the PNV, Herri Batasuna, and other separatist groups in 1998. Urkullu returned to collaboration with a statewide party to ensure his minority government would receive support for everyday matters of governance. Not surprisingly, the areas covered by the pact or alliance which Urkullu established with the Basque Socialists in September 2013 to secure their support in regional and provincial

ambas Administraciones," July 19, 2017, at http://www.lamoncloa.gob.es/serviciosdeprensa/notasprensa/minhap/Paginas/2017/190717-cupo.aspx.

9   For example, "El PNV pide extender el sistema bilateral del concierto a todo el autogobierno vasco," *Deia*, July 10, 2014.

administrations did not include any issues of Basque sovereignty or the region's relationship with Spain—the focus was instead on fiscal reform during a time of economic crisis.

The PNV had thus put its territorial ambitions for some form of sovereignty on the backburner to prioritize other more pressing matters, but they had not been forgotten. Party members suggest that differences within the party during the Ibarretxe period were more to do with questions of speed and timing (i.e., when it is appropriate to take active steps toward this goal, depending on both Basque and Spanish contextual factors) rather than the fundamental essence of the end goal itself.[10] In reality, the PNV still wants to achieve a form of confederal relationship involving cosovereignty with Spain and the right to Basque self-determination, which is much the same as what the Ibarretxe Plan proposed, but this goal has now been re-conceptualized or "re-branded" as seeking a bilateral Political Agreement. While the PNV sees opportunities in the Economic Agreement to extend its bilateral nature to political relations as a basis for confederalism and cosovereignty, it undoubtedly also faces significant obstacles. The following sections analyze the challenges at statewide, supranational, and substate levels to the PNV's territorial ambition.

State-level Challenges

The idea of cosovereignty inherent in the PNV's vision of a bilateral Political Agreement comes up against the same road block that the Ibarretxe Plan hit: that any such proposals are likely to be deemed unconstitutional, since the Spanish Constitution only recognizes one nation (Spain) and invests sole sovereignty in the "Spanish people." Of the four main Spanish parties—the PP, the PSOE, and the two newcomers Ciudadanos (Citizens, C's) and Podemos ("We Can")—only Podemos has shown any inclination to consider changing the Constitution in this regard, while the other three remain firmly committed to sole Spanish sovereignty. If anything, Ciudadanos is even more zealous about national sovereignty than the PP, and certainly it is the first statewide party actively to oppose the existence of the Basque and Navarrese Economic Agreements and to campaign for their dissolution.

---

10   Personal interview with Andoni Ortuzar and Iñaki Goikoetxeta (PNV), April 10, 2014.

There has long been a degree of dissatisfaction in wider Spain about the fact that the Basques (and Navarrese) end up receiving far higher resources per capita through their Economic Agreements than equivalent regions under the common system, since as relatively rich regions they benefit from a system based on their own fiscal capacity. The fact that a detailed breakdown of the figures used to calculate the quota is not published has also served to fuel speculation that Spanish-Basque political deals behind-the-scenes have influenced many of the valuations of competences reached over the years, rather than purely technical and economic arguments.[11] Attention to the disparity in outcomes between the different financing systems grew amidst the financial crisis and the Catalan pro-independence bid, and Ciudadanos saw an opportunity to capitalize on the issue. While the PP and the PSOE have always respected and upheld the Economic Agreement—even if their views on the figures and how to develop the model have often differed from those of the PNV—Ciudadanos has sought to differentiate itself by campaigning against the traditional two-party system in Spain and its heavy reliance on bilateral pacts between minority PP or PSOE governments and regionally-based nationalist parties over the decades. The aforementioned deal the PP struck with the PNV in 2017 in relation to the Economic Agreement, in return for the PNV's support for the 2017 Spanish budget, is precisely the kind of deal Ciudadanos criticizes. At the time of writing this in April 2018, the PNV remains in the position of kingmaker, since the weak minority PP government needs its support, as well as that of Ciudadanos, in order to pass most legislation. The future is nevertheless uncertain, not only in light of the recent strong performance of Ciudadanos in the polls, but of the new multiparty context in the Spanish parliament. If such multipartyism becomes a long-term feature of the Spanish parliament, it is not yet clear what the future might be for traditional mutual support arrangements and pacts between Spanish and regionally based parties.

Attacks against the Basque Economic Agreement itself have thus increased in recent years in reaction to other political and economic circumstances in Spain, which inevitably creates an unfavorable environment for the PNV's goal to extend the bilateral essence of the Economic Agreement to wider political relations too. Animosity toward the Economic Agreement from certain sectors within Spain is well known,

---

11 For a full account of the ins and outs of this debate, see Gray, *Nationalist Politics and Regional Financing Systems*, 112–24.

but far less attention has been paid to the different conceptions of the Economic Agreement even among those who support the model, which also poses hurdles to the PNV's territorial ambition.[12] The remainder of this section seeks to explain this dimension.

Usually, the Basque PP and PSE share the same or similar views as the PNV regarding the finances and development of the Economic Agreement, and so the clashes over the model tend to be between the Spanish authorities and the Basque parties, rather than among parties within the Basque region itself.[13] Thus, the Basque branches of the PP and the PSOE almost always support measures pertaining to the Economic Agreement in the Basque parliament, yet at times these are then rejected by their colleagues in Madrid due to wider implications for other regions in Spain, which can cause internal party contradictions between the Spanish headquarters and Basque branches of the parties. This occurred, for example, in the case of the Shield Law (Ley de Blindaje) designed to upgrade Basque provincial tax regulations to afford them the same legal status as legislation passed by regional or central Spanish governments, a measure supported by the Basque PP but not by the party in Madrid, which voted against the law approved by the PSOE in 2009.[14]

However, clashes over how the Economic Agreement should be developed have also taken place occasionally between the different political parties operating within the Basque region itself, not all of which share exactly the same conceptualization and vision of the Economic Agreement.[15] The PNV and the Basque PP both consider themselves staunch defenders of the Economic Agreement—in the PP's case, due to the historical association between the Spanish right and the historical economic agreements. Yet, they conceive of it differently in some respects. The Basque PP shares the same view as the party's headquarters in Madrid in interpreting the Economic Agreement as a form of fiscal decentralization heavily subject to and subordinate to the Spanish tax system, since the Basque provinces cannot simply create their own taxes and are subject to harmonization rules with Spanish tax

---

12   Caroline Gray, "A Fiscal Path to Sovereignty? The Basque Economic Agreement and Nationalist Politics," *Nationalism and Ethnic Politics* 21, no. 1 (2015), 63–82.

13   The Basque *abertzale* left (see below), however, has always rejected the Economic Agreement, deeming it an insufficient basis for Basque sovereignty. See Xabier Olano's parliamentary intervention, "Mesa Redonda. Viabilidad del Concierto y Convenio Económico en la Europa del siglo XXI," *Azpilcueta* 18 (2002), 309–12.

14   Gray, *Nationalist Politics and Regional Financing Systems*, 154.

15   Ibid., 131–32.

legislation. In consequence, the Basque PP also considers it appropriate that the Spanish government alone should represent the Basques in fiscal matters at European and international level. In contrast, the PNV has come to envisage the Economic Agreement as an instrument of fiscal sovereignty in its own right, which gives the Basques almost the same fiscal powers as Spain or any other EU member state. Ironically, the Basque *abertzale* left[16] shares to some extent the view of the PP, in the sense that it also considers Basque tax legislation strongly subordinate to Spanish legislation, but precisely for this reason it is vehemently against the Economic Agreement, considering the model—and the PNV's allegiance to it—a hindrance to the fullest development of sovereignty that it seeks for the Basque Country.

The roots of these discrepancies in perspective date back to the origins of the Economic Agreement itself. While the PP generally takes the starting point of the Economic Agreement as the first such agreement of 1878 with the Basque provinces spearheaded by their predecessors among the liberal elites and in Araba in particular (a historical stronghold of the Spanish right), the PNV looks further back, remembering the first Economic Agreement as the last vestige of what had originally been a wider set of legal and political rights based on mutual equality governing the relationship between Spain (or previously Castile) and the Basque provinces, known as the *fueros*. The Basque *fueros* were eliminated in 1876 after the Basque provinces had lost the Third Carlist War, and yet the fiscal dimension of the Basque *fueros* was essentially reinstated again two years later by a new arrangement, soon to be named the Economic-Administrative Agreement (Concierto Económico-Administrativo) from 1882 onward, and then simply the Economic Agreement, which would grant the Basque provinces the right to collect taxes again. While the first economic agreement of 1878 did not imply a bilateral pact between equals, the notion of a pact would start to be associated with the Economic Agreement from 1886 onward and would evolve gradually thereafter, echoing the spirit of the original Basque *fueros*.[17] The PP also argues against the PNV's conception of

---

16 "Abertzale" is the Basque for "patriotic." The Basque abertzale left (*izquierda abertale*) is an umbrella term used to denote the various radical left-wing, separatist parties and organizations in the region that have tended to ally together. Aside from their vision of an independent Euskal Herria, they are also known for their anti-capitalist and anti-system ideology.

17 On the historical origins of the Economic Agreement and the concept of a "pact," see Eduardo Alonso Olea, *El Concierto Económico (1878–1937). Orígenes y formación de un Derecho Histórico* (Oñati: Instituto Vasco de Administración Pública (IVAP), 1995).

the Economic Agreement as an instrument of fiscal sovereignty for the Basque region as a whole since the three Basque provinces have only shared an Economic Agreement involving one joint quota payment since 1981. Even among the parties who consider themselves supporters of the Economic Agreement, conceptions of the model and its ultimate aim and purpose thus differ somewhat. The discrepancies pose obstacles to the extension of the PNV's idea of fiscal cosovereignty to political relations too.

SUPRANATIONAL-LEVEL CHALLENGES

This clash in conceptions, between those who consider the Economic Agreement a model of near fiscal sovereignty and those who see it instead as a system of fiscal decentralization subordinate to Spanish legislation, also influences the place of the Basque Economic Agreement within EU fiscal fora.[18] From the turn of the century, one of the main debates over the development of the Economic Agreement became whether the Basques should have a role in EU decision-making bodies debating fiscal matters, particularly those debating tax harmonization between EU member states. Where discrepancies in views have occurred is over the extent to which the Basque authorities should simply adhere to Spanish legislation on the implementation of EU directives and guidance for fiscal harmonization, or whether they should have a more direct voice and participation in EU fiscal decision-making bodies, becoming active players and negotiators in EU tax harmonization processes.

Steps taken by the Basque delegation toward securing Basque representation at EU level over fiscal matters date back to the late 1990s. Only when a minority PSOE government needed the support of the PNV in mid-2010 to approve its 2011 budget did it finally agree to Basque participation in certain working groups of the Economic and Financial Affairs Council (Ecofin) relevant to Basque competences, as part of the Spanish delegation.[19] Legal and technical experts in the provincial treasuries ultimately aspire to go further and achieve co-representation

---

18   Gray, *Nationalist Politics and Regional Financing Systems*, 145–65.
19   Gemma Martínez Bárbara, "La participación de las instituciones vascas en los grupos de trabajo del ECOFIN," in *European inklings (EUi) III. Concierto Económico y Derecho de la Unión Europea*, ed. Isaac Merino Jara and Juan Ignacio Ugartemendia Eceizabarrena (Oñati: Instituto Vasco de Administración Pública (IVAP), 2014), 219.

with the Spanish state representative within the Spanish delegation at Ecofin meetings, rather than solely the working groups, though they recognize that the markedly political character of the Council meetings makes it highly unlikely that the Spanish authorities would agree to such a proposal in the foreseeable future.[20]

Certainly, Spanish-Basque discrepancies in political perspectives on the Economic Agreement, especially on the degree of fiscal autonomy or even sovereignty that it affords, limit the ability of the Basque authorities to develop the Economic Agreement as a model of fiscal sovereignty in Europe to the extent that they would wish. At the same time, however, obstacles to such development—even if the Spanish state were to agree to it without reservation—still persist at EU level. The principle of subsidiarity in force encourages state delegations to take into account regional interests where relevant when forming their position, but the Council is not the place for reflecting internal territorial discrepancies within a member state. This would not be possible for practical reasons; thus, individual regional interests ultimately remain subordinate to the position of the state in its entirety. If the PNV seeks to use the bilateral nature of the Economic Agreement to create a partnership of "equals," and indeed extend this to other areas of Basque-Spanish political relations as part of a new bilateral Political Agreement, this cannot necessarily be easily accommodated in the current EU framework.

The European Union thus offers some opportunities, but also continues to pose a number of obstacles to the development of the kind of "bilateral relationship between equals" within a member state that the PNV seeks. Importantly, however, the fact that the PNV focuses on the Spanish state as the main obstacle to a greater Basque participation at EU level in fiscal and other matters, rather than the EU framework itself, serves to intensify the clash between the PNV's pro-sovereignty territorial agenda and the more centralist vision of most Spanish parties. The clash in political perspectives as to what the prospect of a European fiscal union could mean for the future of the Economic Agreement has been very apparent in the response of PNV representatives to the challenges made by Ciudadanos. PNV spokesperson Josu Erkoreka, for example, has argued that "a fiscal union should be no obstacle to allowing the fiscal and financial powers of the Basques institutions, by virtue of the Economic Agreement, to keep reaching the same level as those afforded by the EU to member states in a new context of increasingly

---

20 Ibid., 231.

limited fiscal sovereignty."[21] This statement is emblematic of the vision of the PNV that the process of increasing fiscal harmonization within the EU should ultimately put the Basque and Spanish treasuries on an equal footing in Europe. In stark contrast, Ciudadanos has argued that fiscal harmonization in Europe will eventually result in specific substate tax systems such as the Basque and Navarrese financing systems becoming "obsolete."[22] These different perspectives have been the source of much controversy.[23]

At present, the issue of developing the Economic Agreement further within the EU context is not an immediately pressing one for the PNV, and debates over questions such as the Basque participation in Ecofin remain primarily at a technical level. The polarization in perceptions as to what opportunities or obstacles the European Union creates for the development of shared sovereignty within a state in fiscal matters and beyond nevertheless points to the challenges that could lie ahead for Spanish-Basque relations amid a European Union in flux.

Substate-level Challenges

Beyond the hurdles at state- and supranational levels, the PNV also faces significant challenges within the Basque region itself to achieving a bilateral Political Agreement. The fundamental dilemma for the PNV remains how to secure a broader consensus within the Basque Country for such a project so that it is not just a nationalist one, in order to avoid the divisions and pitfalls of the Ibarretxe era. In 2013, the PNV launched a parliamentary committee on self-government to investigate possibilities for a new autonomy statute defining a new political relationship with Madrid involving self-determination and cosovereignty, but the committee's progress was slow, and it reached the end of 2015 without any definitive conclusions as to the best way forward, precisely due to the difficulties involved. Since the failure

---

21 Josu Erkoreka, "El Concierto Económico en el contexto de la crisis financiera," personal blog entry, August 5, 2012, at https://josuerkoreka.com/2012/08/05/el-concierto-economico-en-el-contexto-de-la-crisis-financiera/ (my translation). See also "PNV reclama que los poderes fiscales tributarios vascos sigan equiparados a los de estados si se llega a una unión fiscal europea," *Europa Press*, August 5, 2012.

22 For example, "Ciudadanos vuelve a cargar contra el Concierto vasco," *Noticias de Guipúzcoa*, April 5, 2016.

23 For example, "El Gobierno vasco denuncia la ignorancia supina de Ciudadanos sobre el Concierto Económico," *Deia*, April 5, 2016; "Ciudadanos y el PNV se enzarzan por el Concierto," *El Diario Vasco*, April 4, 2016.

of the Ibarretxe Plan, the PNV has been reluctant to take any plan forward that does not have the backing of both the Basque *abertzale* left and the Basque Socialists, to ensure cross-party support spanning the nationalist-statewide divide—a very difficult feat to achieve—as well as strong support from society. While the Socialists' opposition to the idea of self-determination and cosovereignty is well known, this section will focus on the difficulties the PNV also faces in securing support from the Basque *abertzale* left for its proposals.

Following Basque terrorist group ETA's decision to make its ceasefire permanent in 2011, the radical Basque *abertzale* left was able to reenter formal politics under the Bildu coalition from 2011, gaining power for the first (and so far only) time at provincial government level in Gipuzkoa in the provincial elections that year. Batasuna, which had previously been outlawed, was refounded as Sortu and legalized in 2012, becoming the lead party of the coalition, with which the latter was renamed EH Bildu. A key question was how this new situation would impact party alliances in the Basque Country. While the ongoing ramifications of the history of terrorism in the region still conditioned the PNV's political project and the feasibility of nationalist alliances with the Basque *abertzale* left, it also became clear that the PNV and the Basque *abertzale* left were in competition with one another to lead the process of securing a new fit for the Basque Country within or with Spain.

Differences between the PNV and EH Bildu over the Economic Agreement have been particularly evident, which, in turn, has problematized the scope for EH Bildu to agree with the PNV's view of the Economic Agreement as providing a suitable starting point to seek political sovereignty for the Basque Country. EH Bildu's time in power as a minority provisional government in Gipuzkoa in 2011–2015 put the spotlight on these differences.[24] Back in formal politics and in control of the Gipuzkoan treasury, EH Bildu kept up its longstanding criticism of the Economic Agreement as an insufficient basis for Basque sovereignty, in clear contrast to the PNV's praise of the model as the closest current equivalent to the form of "bilateral relationship between equals" that it seeks in wider Spanish-Basque political relations. Certainly, the PNV shares with EH Bildu many of its frustrations over the perceived "limitations" of the Economic Agreement: while both political forces consider it very positive that they have almost full legislative autonomy over direct taxes, they criticize the subordination of the Basque authorities

---

24 Gray, *Nationalist Politics and Regional Financing Systems*, 167–200.

to Spanish legislation in other areas such as indirect taxes, the fight against tax fraud, and other areas of competence crucial to the economy and financial sector, such as financial system regulation, society security, and labor relations.[25] Nevertheless, while the PNV under Urkullu sees these as shortcomings to be gradually improved on, for EH Bildu they are simply evidence that the Economic Agreement is too far removed from its goal of full Basque independence. In the view of Helena Franco, Gizpuzkoan treasury minister for Bildu in the period 2011–2015, "Ultimately, a part of Basque nationalism represented by the PNV seems quite comfortable with the Economic Agreement despite its limitations, while for another, more sovereignty-orientated part of Basque nationalism, it seems clearly insufficient to us to guarantee the future of this country."[26]

The experience of the Basque *abertzale* left entering into formal politics and with a significant political presence, governing at provincial level in Gipuzkoa, also drew attention to the gulf between the PNV and the Basque *abertzale* left on issues of fiscal and economic policy. Under the Economic Agreement, it is the three Basque provinces (known as "historical territories" or "*foral* territories") that are responsible for collecting almost all taxes and for regulating the majority of them, though they must comply with tax harmonization laws with the other provinces as well as with Spanish legislation. Coordination among provinces has worked reasonably well in general since the 1980s, but the past decade has pointed to the pressure that the system can come under at times when different political forces are dominant in different provinces. This has been fundamentally due to opposition from Gipuzkoa to certain tax measures that have nevertheless secured the approval of both Bizkaia and Araba, in large part owing to the longstanding relatively greater weight of left-wing political forces in Gipuzkoa—the Basque Socialists, Eusko Alkartasuna (EA), and the Basque *abertzale* left. Most notably, when Bildu was in power as a minority government at provincial level in Gipuzkoa in the period 2011–2015, it sought to distance itself from the PNV and to carve out a different fiscal vision for the Basque Country, preferring to ally with the Basque federation of a left-wing statewide party (the PSOE) rather than a center-right nationalist party.[27] Thus, it attempted

---

25 The perceived shortcomings of the Economic Agreement listed by Juan José Ibarretxe (PNV) in an interview on October 28, 2014, closely matched those listed by Helena Franco and Xabier Olano (Bildu), interviewed on September 5, 2014, and May 29, 2014, respectively.

26 Personal interview, September 5, 2014 (my translation).

27 For details, see Gray, *Nationalist Politics and Regional Financing Systems*, 194–200.

to seek allies within the PSE in Gipuzkoa to make changes to personal income tax and wealth tax in 2012, and subsequently corporation tax in 2013, which in all cases would have meant higher taxation in Gipuzkoa than in neighboring Bizkaia and Araba.

In turn, this competition on fiscal matters between the PNV and Bildu reduced the scope for them to collaborate on a wider sovereignty agenda for the Basque Country. Bildu sought on many an occasion to stress these differences publically, aiming to differentiate itself clearly from the PNV. PNV representatives, on the other hand, downplayed these differences. For example, they suggested that Bildu overemphasized and even exaggerated its discrepancies with the PNV on fiscal policy as a short-term competition tactic only, but that ultimately it was highly unlikely the Basque *abertzale* left would seek a longer-term social pact with the Socialists, a statewide party, given their incompatibility on the national and territorial question.[28] They also suggested that practical experience of being in government in Gipuzkoa had served to soften the strength of Bildu's anti-capitalist ideology, making it increasingly difficult for the Basque *abertzale* left to claim genuinely that it was carving out a radically different fiscal and social path for the Basque region to that of the PNV.

Ultimately, Bildu's initiatives were thwarted by the regional alliance arrangement and the full fiscal reform pact sealed between the PNV and the PSE at the regional government level in 2013, which also applied to the provinces and was supported too by the PP governing in Araba at the time. This put an end to Bildu-PSE collaboration on fiscal issues in Gipuzkoa, and resulted in the minority Bildu provincial government in Gipuzkoa being outvoted by the PNV, PP, and PSE. A return to a period of relatively more harmonized and harmonious fiscal relations between the three provinces then looked set to ensue from 2015, when the provincial elections put the PNV back in government in all three provinces and resulted in stable PNV-PSE coalition or support arrangements throughout the whole region. A precedent of Bildu-PSE collaboration in Gipuzkoa has nevertheless been set, and the possibility of a degree of collaboration again at some point in the future between left-wing forces in Gipuzkoa, against the PNV, cannot be ruled out. Even if there was perhaps a degree of short-termism in Bildu's behavior, it still revealed the extent to which the Basque abertzale

---

28   For example, personal interview with Joseba Egibar (PNV), April 8, 2014.

left is in strong competition with the PNV, with both seeking to be the dominant political force in the region.

More recent declarations from EH Bildu leaders suggest that they might now be coming around to the idea of reaching a compromise on the PNV's idea of a confederal model as being a "first step" toward EH Bildu's ultimate goal of full independence. In March 2018, Arnaldo Otegi, secretary general of Sortu and figurehead of the Basque *abertzale* left, expressed willingness to explore the idea of a "pact between equals" with Spain as an intermediary solution.[29] At the same time, though, he reiterated the Basque *abertzale* left's rejection of the Economic Agreement as a suitable model for political sovereignty, continuing to argue that EH Bildu considers the model a result of Basque subordination to Spain rather than a genuine pact between equals.

What the future holds is uncertain, and much may also depend on how political shifts underway in wider Spain continue to impact the Basque Country and contribute to shaping political alliances there. During the most recent Basque regional elections in September 2016, the PNV won with a minority of seats in the parliament as usual, but the shift in the political landscape meant that for the first time, parliamentary support from the PSE was not quite enough to give it an absolute majority (it fell one seat short), since the Socialists declined at the hands of left-wing newcomer Podemos. The rise of Podemos in the Basque region from 2015 provided another potential left-wing ally for EH Bildu and one which is further to the left than the PSE, though some of Podemos' success in 2015 and 2016 came at EH Bildu's expense. The future evolution of such developments will contribute to shaping EH Bildu's views on whether to prioritize forming left-wing alliances against the PNV, or territorial alliances with the PNV against statewide parties, or indeed shifting alliances between both possibilities. Certainly, the PNV's ideal goal of securing the backing of *both* the abertzale left and the Basque Socialists for its vision of a bilateral Political Agreement akin to a confederal model still looks a long way from being realized.

---

29 "Ortuzar ve 'realista' instaurar un 'concierto político,'" *Noticias de Álava*, March 2, 2018.

CONCLUDING REMARKS

The Basque Economic Agreement has long provided the fundamental basis for Basque self-government, and its bilateral nature is highly valued by most representatives of the Basque institutions, to the extent that it now provides a prototype for the kind of political cosovereignty with Spain that the PNV seeks. The hurdles to achieving this, however, remain sizeable. Ultimately, much comes down to disputes about sovereignty and where it should lie, which is the fundamental question at the heart of most disagreements between the central Spanish authorities and nationalist parties in the historic regions.

The task of developing the Economic Agreement itself over the years has often been fraught with difficulties, in large part due to the discrepancies between the PNV's vision of the Economic Agreement as a model of fiscal cosovereignty with Spain and desire to develop it as such, in contrast to most Spanish statewide parties' view of the Economic Agreement as a model of fiscal decentralization in which the Basque treasuries should remain subordinate to Spanish legislation. Beyond Spain itself, although the European Union does offer some opportunities for regional participation, the primarily state-centric EU framework cannot easily accommodate the PNV's conception of fiscal or political cosovereignty either. While substate representatives can participate in state delegations at EU Council working groups and meetings, and Bizkaian treasury representatives value their ability to do so in Ecofin working groups, regional interests must ultimately be subordinated to the overriding state position. These dilemmas at state- and supranational levels undoubtedly present hurdles to the feasibility of achieving a wider bilateral Political Agreement too. Meanwhile, on the other hand, the PNV faces an entirely different challenge from EH Bildu, which argues instead that the PNV's idea of political cosovereignty with Spain is not ambitious enough.

These complexities aside, the positives of the Economic Agreement from the Basque perspective have helped to contribute to the continued accommodation of the Basque Country within Spain and to avoid a political and institutional crisis akin to that seen in Catalonia in recent years. Spain undeniably still faces territorial challenges in more than one corner, but nowadays the PNV seeks slower, incremental change, rather than any immediate radical overhaul.

BIBLIOGRAPHY

Alonso Olea, Eduardo. *El Concierto Económico (1878–1937). Orígenes y formación de un Derecho Histórico.* Oñati: Instituto Vasco de Administración Pública (IVAP), 1995.

Field, Bonnie N. "Minority Parliamentary Government and Multilevel Politics: Spain's System of Mutual Back Scratching." *Comparative Politics* 46, no. 3 (2014): 293–312.

Gillespie, Richard. "Between Accommodation and Contestation: The Political Evolution of Basque and Catalan Nationalism." *Nationalism and Ethnic Politics* 21, no. 1 (2015), 3–23.

Gray, Caroline. *Nationalist Politics and Regional Financing Systems in the Basque Country and Catalonia.* Bilbao: Foral Treasury Doctoral Thesis Collection, 2016. At http://www.conciertoeconomico. org/phocadownload/TESIS-Gray-Nationalists-politics.pdf .

———. "A Fiscal Path to Sovereignty? The Basque Economic Agreement and Nationalist Politics." *Nationalism and Ethnic Politics* 21, no. 1 (2015): 63–82.

Keating, Michael, and Zoe Bray. "Renegotiating Sovereignty: Basque Nationalism and the Rise and Fall of the Ibarretxe Plan." *Ethnopolitics* 5, no. 4 (2006), 347–64.

Martínez Bárbara, Gemma. "La participación de las instituciones vascas en los grupos de trabajo del ECOFIN." In *European inklings (EUi) III. Concierto Económico y Derecho de la Unión Europea*, edited by Isaac Merino Jara and Juan Ignacio Ugartemendia Eceizabarrena. Oñati: Instituto Vasco de Administración Pública (IVAP), 2014. At

http://www.conciertoeconomico.org/joomdocs/autores/IVAP-2014_MARTINEZ-G_La-participacion-de-las-Instituciones-Forales-en-el-ECOFIN.pdf.

Olano, Xabier. Parliamentary intervention. In "Mesa Redonda. Viabilidad del Concierto y Convenio Económico en la Europa del siglo XXI." *Azpilcueta* 18 (2002), 307–18. http://www.euskomedia. org/PDFAnlt/azpilcueta/18/18307318.pdf.

Chapter 7

The Impact of
the Basque Economic Agreement on
Community Economic Development

Sofía Arana Landín[1]

The Economic Agreement is a pact between the Basque Country and the rest of Spain that has deep roots in the Basque *foral* system, dating back to the thirteenth century when the Basque provincial councils joined Castile.

According to Ignacio Zubiri,[2] until 1876 these territories had charters that provided them with ample autonomy and in particular with the possibility of raising their own taxes. Even when these charters were abolished, the tax autonomy continued for the provincial councils of Bizkaia and Gipuzkoa through Economic Agreements until Franco's dictatorship in 1936. The historical territory of Araba maintained its

1   I hereby thank Dr. John Mollenkopf for his kind invitation and support. I have to give very special thanks to Rebecca Lurie at the CUNY Murphy Institute and director of the "Worker Ownership Project," who has been the main pillar of it all. Always with an incredible disposition she has introduced me to great people working on cooperativism, like Chris Adams, from the Legal Clinic at CUNY Law, Chris Michael from ICA, Maggie Marron at the Urban Justice Center, and Carmen Huertas-Noble, Director of the Community and Economic Development Clinic, at the CUNY Law School, and so many others that I cannot name, but I thank them all. Special thanks to Tiffany Collins for her kind suggestions. I also want to thank the Public Advocate, Letitia James team, and Birch Ha Pam for kindly listening to our ideas and looking for ways to put them into practice in New York City and devoting their time and effort to do so; DER2015-63533-C4-1-P (MINECO/FEDER); GIC 15/08 from the Basque government.
2   Ignacio Zubiri Oria, *The Economic Agreement between the Basque Country and Spain* (Bilbao: Ad concordiam, 2014), 15.

Economic Agreement even during Franco's dictatorship. I am not going to delve into this history, which has already been studied by many researchers,[3] because I want to focus on one particular outcome.

The Economic Agreement is based on the principles of liability and fiscal autonomy with the payment of a quota equivalent to the state's expenses in the Basque Country.

This fiscal autonomy can be seen at the subnational level, where the three provinces legislate about tax matters separately and with autonomy and raise taxes accordingly. However, they pay the quota jointly.

Thus, within this particular system, the decisions of the provincial authorities, democratically deciding upon the taxes to be raised among the citizens, was probably a major feature of Basque history and the basis of the current system. This fact leads to public policies being held very dear to the citizen, as in the old times when "equality, solidarity, love for the environment and social progress" were already in our ancestors' minds. This can be regarded as the key of today's success in entities such as cooperatives investing in CSR (corporate social responsibility). As Mikel Lezamiz, the director of Mondragon Corporation dissemination unit, has stated: "Our mission is not to earn money, it is to create wealth within society through entrepreneurial development and job creation." It seems that traditional values are still equally important today, providing a stable basis for a peculiar socioeconomic model through times.

Thus, the Economic Agreement has provided us with unique roots. The way of raising revenue in the Basque Country—with the principles of equality, solidarity, preservation of the environment, and social progress in mind—has only been possible thanks to our capacity to legislate and raise taxes, which in turn are a result of the Economic Agreement.

Each region has unique features that have contributed to the development of a specific economic model. In the case of the Basque Country, thanks to the Economic Agreement, cooperativism can be said to be a key feature, as this form of enterprise becomes particularly relevant both in numbers and in social and economic power, particularly in the historical territory of Gipuzkoa. Moreover, the Basque Country has proven to be one of the leading regions in research and innovation

---

3   See, among others, Joseba Agirreazkuenaga, *The Making of the Basque Question* (Reno: Center for Basque Studies, University of Nevada, Reno, 2011); Joseba Agirreazkuenaga and Eduardo Alonso Olea, *The Basque Fiscal System: History, Current Status, and Future Perspectives* (Reno: Center for Basque Studies, University of Nevada, Reno, 2014).

in the European Union, a fact that has also contributed decisively to the success of this model.

If we delve into the possible factors that have contributed to this success, we cannot find just one that can be said to be "the one and only." It is probably a confluence of all possible factors (historical, cultural, legal, and public policies) that has contributed to this model. However, all this would not have been possible without the Economic Agreement.

The Basque Country's Statute of Autonomy (Organic Law 3/1979 of December 18) in article 10 recognizes the exclusive competence of this community regarding the social economy (SE): cooperatives, mutual societies, fishermen's associations, associations, and foundations. Therefore, the Basque government and the provincial governments have the task of promoting these sorts of entities.

The strength of the Basque Country's SE movement comes particularly from the cooperative movement, its greatest exponent being the "Mondragon: Humanity at Work Cooperative Group."[4] This group has become an important reference point for researchers in social economy as an example of a self-regulating economy. As Greg McLeod[5] states:

> ...in analyzing the Mondragon complex in terms of their own particular interests, these writers have neglected a crucial element, namely its basis in Judeo-Christian values. For example, writers have discussed the experience in the light of the British labour movement, in the light of French cooperative history, in terms of the Marxist tradition and in one enlightening work, comparing the strategies with those of Mahatma Ghandi.

A MAJOR INVESTMENT IN CSR AS A CONSEQUENCE OF THE ECONOMIC AGREEMENT

As well as "corporate social performance," CSR implies "responsible business," "corporate responsibility," "corporate citizenship," and "sustainable responsible business," and it has become one of the most important aspects of managing right a business in the twenty-first

---

4   Previously known as MCC (Mondragón Cooperative Corporation).
5   Greg McLeod, *From Mondragon to America* (Cape Breton, Nova Scotia: University College of Cape Breton Press, 1997), 14.

century. In the European Union, CSR now is evident in Europe 2020 (especially new skills and jobs, youth, local development), business and human rights, CSR reporting, and recently, socially responsible public procurement.

The Economic Agreement also has implications for CSR, as neither educational nor environmental or social problems can be effectively tackled without the close involvement of the community and its individuals. Thanks to the cultural values and the possibility of promoting them in an autonomous way, educational and environmental effectiveness as well as sustainable development have been effectively reached. It is in this context that the concern for so-called corporate social responsibility becomes a main issue, a form of business self-regulation.

However, it is also true that regulations change depending on the social conscience of the time. There had been certain issues that were not regulated by law in the past and, thanks to a growing social consciousness, have ended up being regulated. Some clear examples of this would be environmental issues, workers' rights, gender equality, and so forth. This leads us to the conclusion that some of CSR functions that are self-regulated today will probably become regulated by law in a near future, but CSR will always take the lead and have its own self-regulated corpora.

This is what has happened with cooperatives, which have enshrined CSR for decades because of an altruistic sense of community. Thus, this fact is born in mind by legislators in determining their own policies so that these altruistic, community-oriented entities can receive special tax treatment thanks to the Economic Agreement.

Cooperatives and other social economy entities in the Basque Country have taken on commitments to solve socially important and general interest problems, making an effective contribution to economic growth but with fairer income and wealth distribution. This could be a reason for the sustainable success of a very particular cooperative model in the Basque Country, of which Mondragon is without doubt its greatest exponent.

Key Features of the Success of the "Mondragon: Humanity at Work Cooperative Group" System

The "Mondragon: Humanity at Work Cooperative Group" is the major exponent of a highly democratic and successful socioeconomic initiative integrated by autonomous and independent cooperatives in which CSR plays a key role. This corporation is located in the province of Gipuzkoa, having deep cultural roots in the Basque Country, but it has expanded to over fifty other countries.

One of its features is reflected in its name—"Humanity at Work Cooperative Group," as it was created for and by people and inspired by the basic principles of cooperativism. This entrepreneurial complex is the result of the historical process of integration of the cooperatives related to the Mondragon experience, boosted by its founder, Jose Maria Arizmendiarrieta, and studied worldwide.[6]

Its founder´s vision of a worthwhile human society is characterized by the virtues of survival: solidarity and work;[7] he believed that "the emancipation of a class or of people must begin with the training of those who make it up," so education and training was important from the very beginning in order to be able to work and make the change happen. Thus, in August 1943, he launched the Arrasate-Mondragón Professional School in order to democratize labor to help humble young people improve their education as a means for better employment opportunities. No wonder that nowadays Basque cooperatives are usually highly innovative, providing research, products, and services, with particular importance given to innovation, research, and development.

The management communitarian model is based on the individual and their satisfaction, with the aim of achieving total quality. These structures become a very flexible instruments to adapt to different contexts, such as economic crises or particularly high demand for a product.

Regarding cooperatives' economic flexibility, when times are bad, workers and owners can cut wage costs by negotiating among themselves

---

6 See, among others, Jaroslav Vanek, *The Participatory Economy: An Evolutionary Hypothesis and a Strategy for Development* (Ithaca, NY: Cornell University-ILR Press, 1975); Henk Thomas and Chris Logan, *Mondragon: An Economic Analysis* (London: Allen and Unwin, 1982); William Whyte and King White, *Making Mondragon: The Growth and Dynamics of the Worker Cooperative Complex* (Ithaca, NY: Cornell University-ILR Press, 1988).

7 See McLeod, *From Mondragon to America*, 57.

and, owners can also forsake dividends. Furthermore, when a cooperative within the group has money left over, and another cooperative has run out, they can lend one another money. Another example of this flexibility is when a cooperative within the group has an excess of members, they can relocate them to other cooperatives within the group that may need those workers.

This way, the cooperatives within the group, thanks to the principle of inter-solidarity, can be said to be more flexible and thus resilient at bad times. The system is adaptable to changing social needs and circumstances. However, we cannot forget the very long tradition of neighborhood work cooperatively or *auzolan* in Basque culture.

Within the group, the individual cooperatives contribute financially to the corporation's development, exchange staff (particularly as an alternative to redundancies in one business), and jointly establish Mondragon's strategy. This is done through the Co-operative Congress (650 delegates, representing each member firm) and the general council it appoints. This last cooperative group can be regarded as a democratic federation formed by cooperatives of different kinds. The totality ends up being a lot bigger than its parts.

THE INFLUENCE OF THE ECONOMIC AGREEMENT ON THE BASQUE COUNTRY'S COOPERATIVE SUBSTANTIVE REGULATION

Thanks to the Economic Agreement there are a series of public policies coming from both the Basque government and the provincial governments that have helped create the foundations for these cooperative movements.

Three different administrations can promote different policies depending on the subject matter. Basically, the state is in charge of taking measures for the promotion of these entities within the areas of work, employment, and social welfare, while the Basque government uses other types of aid, and the foral governments are in charge of tax policies regarding these entities.

Thus, the Basque government has a specific Directorate for Cooperatives and a Council of Cooperatives. At present the Directorate of Social Economy[8] within the Department of Employment and Social

---

8   According to Decree 315/2005 of October 18 and to Decree 4/2009 (BOPV No. 141, June 23, 2009), the Department of Justice, Employment,

Affairs manages the Cooperative Register and labor companies and their inspection and control; the training and aid programs to promote all sort of entities within the social and solidarity economy, offering grants to promote and develop inter-cooperation. This way, several important structures have been established, creating greater added value for cooperatives and making the processes of creation and development of cooperatives a lot easier.[9] As a result, there is the Council of Cooperatives that provides consultation about the promotion and dissemination of cooperativism.

The Basque public institutions have full competence in cooperative matters, as can be seen in the 4/1993 Bill of Cooperatives in the Basque Country. Thus, some differences with the general legislation can be found. As a whole, company law requirements for cooperatives are stricter than under the general legislation, but there is an important difference in the Basque Country: there is no need to separate cooperative results from extracooperative ones, thus facilitating accountancy and reducing internal costs.

Cooperatives in the Basque Country do have a different substantive legislation than other sort of entities, which requires them to make greater efforts and prevents them from acting as capitalist enterprises.

Note that the provincial governments are fully competent to legislate over most taxes; in particular, both personal income tax and corporate income tax legislative and applicative powers belong to each of the provincial governments. In this way, the provincial governments have a clear voice to say in this matter.

The 4/1993 Bill on Cooperatives ensures democratic values in different aspects such as the distribution of the net surplus, as there are very strict norms that regulate it. First of all, 20 percent of the yearly

---

and Social Welfare was terminated and the Office of Social Economy became new name Office of Social Economy, Social, and Entrepreneurial Responsibility.

9   There are also several entities created for the purpose of helping cooperatives from their creation throughout their existence, including Elkar-Lan, S. Coop., a second-degree cooperative established in 2003 by the Council of Cooperatives of the Basque Country, the Confederation of Cooperatives in the Basque Country, and the Federation of Cooperatives of Associated Work, Teaching and Credit in the Basque Country for the creation of employment within cooperatives; Oinarri, S.G.R., a mutual guarantee society invested in, among others, by the Council of Cooperatives of the Basque Country.

net surplus must be assigned to the Compulsory Reserve Fund in order to consolidate, develop, and guarantee the cooperative.

This fund cannot be transferred to members, even if they leave, by any means, as it can only be used to pay debts. This is extremely useful because it avoids "mules" so that it lasts for the subsequent generations or provides assurance to third parties, so that, for instance, lenders know that cooperatives have this fund, which means they are financially stronger than a normal corporation. The fund is mostly devoted to paying loses at times of crisis, and it is a major factor in cooperatives' resilience. It also impedes speculation; even though the cooperative might be very strong, the resources in this fund are not worthwhile to speculators.

Second, another 10 percent of the net surplus needs to be assigned to the Education and Promotion Fund for the contribution for education and cooperative promotion and other areas of public interest, like the environment. This is how the cooperative returns the investment to the community. Besides offering courses and training for workers, they also usually donate to nongovernmental organizations (NGOs), charity, environmental causes, or helping other cooperatives in need.

The same is true of the Compulsory Reserve Fund; the amounts in the Education Fund cannot be distributed among members under any circumstances; if the cooperative did so, it would lose its "fiscal protection" and would then have to use the general tax system. In addition, these reserves cannot be seized, as even in the event of closure the amounts are assigned to a public institution whose objective is to help other cooperatives. Thus, 30 percent of the yearly net surplus is never going to revert to members, economically speaking, even if the cooperative became extinguished.

Third, within the cooperative, the general assembly must allocate the remaining 70 percent. The bill offers three different options: paying patronage refunds, creating voluntary reserve funds, or distributing it among workers.

Out of this 70 percent, very often a percentage is retained by the cooperative to be used to benefit the "common good" of the cooperative (research, development, innovation, job creation, and so on), and the balance of the profits goes into capital accounts for the worker owners. These funds may be borrowed against at the cooperative's bank at very low interest rates and are important parts of the social welfare arrangements. The cooperatives acknowledge a duty to contribute to the common good by reinvesting a high proportion of their profits, including regular investments in community funds for job creation; taking care of their social welfare, unemployment, and health insurance requirements (through a cooperative owned by other cooperatives called Lagun Aro); and being active in their community.

In any case, 30 percent of the yearly net surplus devoted to Compulsory Reserve Funds can be regarded as a tax and, as we are going to see, this is the main reason for their having a particular tax system.

But this particular tax system also derives from objective reasons for their promotion as, among other things (as we have seen), they have a lower capacity to compete on the market because of their inherent legal obligations and characteristics (in relation to the ability to pay principle); their contribution to the general interest has proven to have benefited the local community in which they are inserted, creating steady jobs and investing locally; they provide opportunities for groups that would otherwise be excluded (as for instance the cooperatives for disabled people); and with respect to the creation of new companies, worker cooperatives have generally behaved in a more dynamic way during the last forty years than the rest of the economy in the Basque Country.

All this is reflected in the evolution of the relative influence of the gross added value generated by the social economy on the gross domestic product of the Basque Country's economy as a whole, which has increased over recent years[10] and is the highest in Spain.

Employment in this sector means a 6.8 percent of the whole of the Basque Country, generating 5.8 percent of the gross added value. Furthermore, an examination of the gross capital formation of the Basque social economy reveals figures that are superior to those of the rest of the economy.

THE ECONOMIC AGREEMENT AND PUBLIC POLICIES IN RELATION THE CORPORATE INCOME TAX FOR COOPERATIVES

As we have previously explained, the foral Entities of the Basque Country have practically full competence in the field of taxation within the taxes that are in the Basque Economic Agreement with the state. The most

---

10 Note that the information shown refers exclusively to the sector of cooperatives.

important tax for cooperatives is corporate income tax, and its regulation can be considered to be the main public policy for cooperativism, as cooperatives have their own special regime.

First, in order to compensate cooperatives for the compulsory allocations they have to make to reserves, all cooperatives can deduct from taxable income 50 percent of the amounts dedicated to the Compulsory Reserve Fund and the whole amount devoted to the Education and Promotion Fund.

I find this a very important fact for their promotion, as it forces the cooperatives to save for a rainy day. Thus, as their higher substantive requirements impede partners-workers to get the full amount of the profits, taxation is adapted to them, considering this fact as a sort of tax for cooperatives. It is only logical that they have their own Corporate Income Tax Bill in which these issues are taken into account.

For small and medium-sized cooperatives, the tax rate is an 18 percent, in comparison to a 22 percent rate for other legal entities, like the most typical forms of capitalist entities. For the rest, those who cannot qualify as small of medium-sized cooperatives have a 20 percent tax rate, while other entities have a 26 percent. However, there is now a minimum tax rate of a 10.75 percent for cooperatives and other entities. Specially privileged cooperatives have a 50 percent tax rebate on top of this. These tax perks can be considered an adaptation to their circumstances in terms of compulsory reserve funds and investment in the community.

THE ADMINISTRATION'S SUBSIDY POLICIES

The Directorate of Social Economy establishes different policies in order to promote it. To begin with, there are different forms of aid for the establishment of entities belonging to the sector, its main goal being to create new entities.

For their growth, there are different forms of aid devoted to education and training, such as the educational and training aid for the stimulation of the social and solidarity economy and the different grants and subsidies for studies and research in the field of the social and solidarity economy.

There is also aid for the consolidation of social and solidarity economy entities. It subsidizes different activities such as the cost of structures for the maintenance and consolidation of associative entities, with a view to fulfilling the legal objectives assigned and aid for technical assistance and the promotion of professionalized management for social and solidarity economy entities, such as the possible implementation of management plans and advice for strategic plans and marketing plans, particularly for small and medium-sized social and solidarity economy entities. There is also aid to promote investments in social and solidarity economy entities with fewer than ten employees. This aid is specifically concerned with financing part of the interests generated from the loans granted for making investments.

There is also great interest in the creation of bigger structures so that, according to the principles of solidarity and inter-cooperation, entities associate and become stronger. Aid for entrepreneurial inter-cooperation in the social economy helps to achieve this aim. It can greatly reduce costs, not only because they have to share, but also because they become subsidized. For instance, they partake in and benefit from various studies for new lines of products, the unification of services, joint acquisition of new technologies, joint financing mechanisms, marketing agreements, mergers, and so on.

There is also aid to enable workers and unemployed people to participate in social economy enterprises, such as the incorporation of employed persons as partners, the implementation of instruments in favor of the financial participation of new worker-partners, and the implementation of tools in order to promote CSR.

As we can see, cooperatives, being social economy entities, can have access to all sorts of aid, from their creation to their education and growth. According to the ability to pay principle, the smaller entities are protected and provided for. Thus, this whole system complies with our legal system that obliges its promotion.

SUCCESS FACTORS TO KEEP IN MIND

A few characteristics of the system that can be considered to be success factors can be pointed out.

Certain factors can contribute to success, such as the initial capital of 3,000 euros, which can be regarded as quite a low amount. Note that this amount is shared among members and that there are no other expenses, as they are excluded from the taxes for their creation and their inscription in the register. Another factor that helps them in their creation is the fact that there are no-interest loans. Moreover, creation is a guided process, and free advice for their creation and technical assistance are provided in the start-up phase and, very often, throughout their lifetimes.

The main success factor that helps to consolidate and strengthens cooperatives and increases their resilience is probably the Compulsory Reserve Fund. Even though compliance with the allocation of a 20 percent of the net surplus to this fund can seem burdensome, in the long run, it is what makes the cooperatives strong and resilient, and it helps raise them in the regard of possible lenders.

From the very beginning of the cooperatives' existence, education was the key to helping workers to cope with the different demands throughout the cooperative's life. This is why the Compulsory Education and Promotion Fund makes cooperatives invest in education and training, innovation, and so on. This way, the cooperative becomes more flexible to the market, and worker owners are better able to fulfill their mission. Different aid in the form of grants and subsidies from the Directorate of Social Economy is also devoted to fulfilling this purpose.

In terms of synergies, inter-cooperation is also a success factor. For this purpose, the Directorate of Social Economy promotes the small and medium-sized entities in particular, incentivizing their integration in bigger structures, such as federations, associations, second-degree cooperatives, mergers, consortia, and so on. This fact helps them become stronger and reduces all sorts of costs in education, training, innovation, technical support, access to funding, and so on.

We cannot forget that "Mondragon: Humanity at Work" is a corporation made up of 120 different cooperatives that help and assist each other within the group. Through the transfer of funds, workers, and innovation, all cooperatives within the group become stronger. The principle of inter-cooperation also provides them with the importance attributed to economies of scale. Thus, they are taken seriously by all other economic and political agents.

Conclusions

The Economic Agreement has had a very deep impact on the socioeconomic system of the Basque Country as, for centuries, educational, social, environmental, and economic issues have been addressed closely thanks to a very high level of autonomy.

The Economic Agreement has had a direct impact on community economic development. Thus, cooperatives in the Basque Country are considered to be particularly resilient and successful. Notwithstanding, it is not only cooperatives who benefit from this system, but society as a whole. The reason for this is that, under the right circumstances, cooperatives are highly productive, taking care of the environment and creating jobs and wealth for the whole society, and being a maximum exponent of CSR locally.

CSR in the Basque Country can be said to be particularly developed, as many entities belong to the social economy and thus these principles and values direct them, as self- regulation in terms of CSR can be said to be more advanced than in other entities.

In the Basque Country and most particularly in Gipuzkoa, where the Mondragon group is located, many historical factors that have contributed to a very peculiar model based on a network of social economy entities, particularly in the form of cooperatives.

The reserve funds cooperatives in the Basque Country are indivisible and nontransferable in order to protect the cooperative from speculation and to make these funds stay in the cooperative for the community and future generations, so they can be regarded as a tax. In this way, cooperatives are already contributing to the community, so there is a need for public policies for them in return, both from the supply and from the demand side.

Thanks to the deep historical roots of the Basque Country and to the autonomy granted by the Economic Agreement, it has a democratic system of access from workers to capital that has proven to be reliable and successful.

BIBLIOGRAPHY

Agirreazkuenaga, Joseba. *The Making of the Basque Question*. Reno: Center for Basque Studies, University of Nevada, Reno, 2011.

———, and Eduardo Alonso Olea. *The Basque Fiscal System: History, Current Status, and Future Perspectives*. Reno: Center for Basque Studies, University of Nevada, Reno, 2014.

Alperovitz, Graham. *Principles of a Pluralistic Commonwealth*. Washington, D.C.: The Democracy Collaborative, 2017.

Arnold, N. Scott. "Further Thoughts on the Degeneration of Market Socialism: A Reply to Schweickart." *Economics and Philosophy* 3, no. 2 (1987): 320–30.

Artz, Georjeanne, and Yun Kim. "Business Ownership by Workers: Are Worker Cooperatives a Viable Option?" Iowa State University Working Papers, Working Paper 11020, 2011.

Bakaikoa, Baleren, and Eneka Arbizu, eds. *Basque Cooperativism*. Reno: Center for Basque Studies, University of Nevada, Reno, 2011.

Basterrechea Markaida, Imanol. "Sources of Competitive Advantage in the Mondragon Cooperative Group." In *Basque Cooperativism*, edited by Baleren Bakaikoa and Eneka Albizu. Reno: Center for Basque Studies, University of Nevada, Reno, 2011.

Borja Álvarez, Antón. "Innovation in the Basque Country: An Examination of the Cooperative Situation." In *Basque Cooperativism*, edited by Baleren Bakaikoa and Eneka Albizu. Reno: Center for Basque Studies, University of Nevada, Reno, 2011.

Bradley, Keith, and Alan Gelb. *Worker Capitalism: The New Industrial Relations*. London: Heinemann, 1983.

CECOP. *Social Cooperatives and Social and Participative Enterprises* (CECOP- CICOPA). Brussels: CECOP, 2012.

Cerrato Allende, Javier. "Culture and Social Representations of Work among Basques: Implications for Organizational Commitment and cooperative Attitudes." In *Basque Cooperativism*, edited by Baleren Bakaikoa and Eneka Albizu. Reno: Center for Basque Studies, University of Nevada, Reno, 2011.

Chaves, Rafael, and Danielle Demoustier. *The Emergence of the Social Economy in Public Policy: An International Analysis*. Brussels: Peter Lang, 2013.

Dow, Gregory K., ed. *Governing the Firm: Workers Control in Theory and in Practice*. Cambridge, UK and New York: Cambridge University Press, 2003.

Ellerman, David. "Workers' Cooperatives: The Question of Legal Structure." In *Worker Cooperatives in America*, edited by Robert Jackall and Henry M. Levin. Berkeley: University of California Press, 1984.

———, and Peter Pitegoff. "The Democratic Corporation: The New Worker Cooperative Statute in Massachusetts." *New York University Review of Law and Social Change* 9, no. 3 (1983): 441–72.

Fernández de Bobadilla Güemez, Sara, and Eva Velasco Balmaseda. "Is Innovation Better Managed by Corporations than Social Economy Companies? A Comparative Study of Innovative Basque Companies." In *Basque Cooperativism*, edited by Baleren Bakaikoa and Eneka Albizu. Reno: Center for Basque Studies, University of Nevada, Reno, 2011.

Hansmann, Henry. *The Ownership of Enterprise*. Boston: Belknap Press, 2000.

Henk, Thomas, and Chris Logan. *Mondragon: An Economic Analysis*. London: Allen and Unwin, 1982.

Huertas Noble, Carmen. "Worker-owned and Unionized Worker-Owned Cooperatives: Two Tools to Address Income Inequality." *Clinical Law Review* 22, no. 2. (2016): 325–58.

McLeod, Greg. *From Mondragon to America*. Cape Breton, Nova Scotia: University College of Cape Breton Press, 1997.

Monzon, José Luis, and Rafael Chaves. "The European Social Economy: Concept and Dimensions of the Third Sector." *Annals of Public and Cooperative Economics* 79, nos. 3–4 (2008): 549–77.

Oakeshott, Ralph. "'Grass Roots' Enterprises Thrive Amid the Basques." *The Financial Times*, July 9, 1973.

———. "Mondragon: Spain's Oasis of Democracy." *The Observer*, January 21, 1976.

Olson, Mancur. *The Logic of Collective Action: Public Goods and the Theory of Groups.* Harvard Economic Studies 124. Cambridge, MA: Harvard University Press, 1971.

Pérez de Uralde, José María, Baleren Bakaikoa, et al. *Social Economy and Social Participation: The Ways of the Basques.* Madrid: Marcial Pons, 1996.

Riley-Duff, Rory. "Communitarian Governance in Social Enterprises: Case Evidence from the Mondragon Cooperative Corporation and School Trends Ltd." *Social Enterprise Journal* 6, no. 2 (2010): 125–45.

Rothschild, Joyce. "Workers' Cooperative and Social Enterprise: A forgotten Route to Social Equity and Democracy." *American Behavioral Scientist* 52 (2009): 1023–25.

Schweickart, David. *Against Capitalism.* Chicago: Westview Press, 1996.

———. *After Capitalism (New Critical Theory).* Chicago: Westview Press, 2002.

Thomas, Henk, and Chris Logan. *Mondragon: An Economic Analysis.* London: Allen and Unwin, 1982.

Vanek, Jaroslav. *The Participatory Economy: An Evolutionary Hypothesis and a Strategy for Development.* Ithaca, NY: Cornell University-ILR Press, 1975.

Whyte, William, and King Whyte. *Making Mondragon: The Growth and Dynamics of the Worker Cooperative Complex.* Ithaca, NY: Cornell University-ILR Press, 1988.

Zubiri Oria, Ignacio. *The Economic Agreement between the Basque Country and Spain.* Bilbao: Ad Concordiam, 2014.

Chapter 8

Federalism and the Cities of the
Twenty-First Century

Roberto Bernales Soriano

THE REVIVAL OF CITIES AS THE NEW MAIN CHARACTERS IN THE GLOBAL ECONOMY

The "modern" agglomeration of the population in the cities started with the Industrial Revolution and since then has not stopped. When analyzing the phenomena, we should not forget the evolution of the urban development under two broad perspectives: the perspective of the developed world through the end of the nineteenth and the whole twentieth century, and the perspective of the cities of developing countries (that is, most of the African and Asian countries) in which the population live crowded together in all sort of slums. In any case, the common feature of the cities is that they are all groups of population that do not produce by themselves their means to survive,[1] so they are by definition not capable of being self-sufficient.

The steady economic growth experimented through the twentieth and beginning of the twenty-first centuries created a false belief among the urbanites that the risks of uncontrolled growth could be solved by never-ending technological and scientific developments. We currently know that we have to take action to tackle environmental (climate change, the lack of drinkable water, deforestation) and social (urbanization

---

1   See Francois Ascher, *Los nuevos principios del urbanismo* (Madrid: Alianza, 2004).

demands, aging population) urbanization challenges that our planet and cities especially face in our times and will face in the near future. More than twenty-five years ago (during the Rio de Janeiro summit of 1992), it was said that the battle for the sustainability of the planet would be won or lost in the cities. Those were the days in which "glocalization" became a new concept by which we should think global and act locally.[2]

On the other hand, and parallel to the existing urbanization process that started in the twenty-first century, another phenomenon has arisen in recent years. Economies of the First World are becoming more urbanized and technological innovation is more and more concentrated in urban innovation hubs.[3] There is a resurgence of city centers due to a new class of creative "knowledge workers." This was predicted more than fifteen years ago,[4] but the subsequent consequences such as gentrification, inequality, and economic segregation were unforeseeable. The economic crisis has strengthened both the revival of the cities and the disturbing consequences it brings, but the urban crisis is not just an urban crisis; it is a crisis of knowledge-based capitalism.[5]

In political terms, it has been argued that in a changing and ungovernable world cities, not states, will be the "islands of governance on which the future world order will be built."[6] The World Economic Forum also focused on the importance of the cities the new economic order wherein decentralization of governance to regional and local bodies is a megatrend that will shape the twenty-first century.[7]

All those things considered plus economic shocks, the increasing precarious nature of employment, globalized markets, and the information flow that citizens manage in order to control the accountability of their

2   Antonio Lucio Gil, "Ciudades: El escenario en el que nos jugamos el future," Cambio climático: El Planeta Atormentado 18, suppl., *eldiario.es* (online newspaper), April 2, 2018.

3   Robin Boadway and Sean Dougherty, *Decentralisation in a Globalised World: Consequences and Opportunities*, OECD Working Papers on Fiscal Federalism, no. 21 (Paris: OECD, 2018), 3–14.

4   Richard Florida, *The Rise of the Creative Class: And How It's Transforming Work, Leisure, Community and Everyday Life* (New York: Basic Books, 2002).

5   See the interview with Richard Florida in John Battelle, "Can Business and New Federalism Save our Cities?" *Newco Shift*, September 14, 2017, at https://shift. newco.co/can-business-and-new-federalism-save-our-cities-e5926997f578.

6   McKinsey Global Institute, *When Cities Rule the World* (2014), quoted in Véronique Herry-Saint-Onge, Morvan Le Borgne, Jesse Kancir, Emilie Nicolas, André Juneau, and James Stuewe, *Empowered Cities: A New Path to Collaborative Federalism* (N.p.: Action Canada, 2015), 4–18.

7   World Economic Forum, *The Competiveness of Cities* (2014), quoted in Herry-Saint-Onge et al., *Empowered Cities*, 4.

representatives have important consequences for both unitary and decentralized states.[8] The challenges imply that we should reconsider and test again the advantages and disadvantages of decentralization in general, and federalism in particular, and their influences on globalization (and vice versa), taking into account these new elements of urbanization and information innovation. And we should not forget that decentralization seems to encourage economic growth in highly open economies, but it also brings economic inequality.[9]

In any case, the nature and extent of decentralization should be tested against the phenomena of globalization. This new setting is accompanied by the increased movement of people to large urban areas and the efforts of these areas to attract knowledge-based production activities that, in turn, imply challenges from fiscal and tax perspectives. Further, the new forms of information technology empower citizens to control their representatives, which may also bring a more efficient service delivery and reduction of costs of citizens transacting with their governments, especially local ones, and a greater awareness of what other jurisdictions do, leading to more competition and innovation (yardstick competition).[10] The consequence is a reinforcement of local governments, together with the assumption of the federal government of responsibilities of state (or regional) governments due to the pressure of globalization on the later ones.[11]

FEDERALISM AND LOCAL GOVERNMENTS

Federal systems are usually conceived, although not exclusively so, as comprising two orders of government: federal and state (the latter referring to states, provinces, *Länder*, and cantons). Local government is usually seen as a competence of states, implying that the primary

---

8 Boadway and Dougherty, *Decentralisation in a Globalised World.*
9 Sean M. Dougherty and Oguzhan Akgun, "Globalisation, Decentralization and Inclusive Growth," in *Fiscal Decentralisation and Inclusive Growth,* ed. Sean M. Dougherty and Junghun Kim (Paris: OECD/KPF, 2018).
10 The theory of political yardstick competition states that a comparison of public service levels and tax rates with those in nearby jurisdictions can provide voters with a useful instrument to assess politicians' performance. However, we argue that fiscal disparities bias this yardstick, and that this bias may be removed through fiscal equalization. See Maarten A. Allers, "Yardstick Competition, Fiscal Disparities, and Equalization," *Economics Letters* 117, no. 1 (2012), 4–6, at https://econpapers.repec.org/article/eeeecolet/v_3a117_3ay_3a2012_3ai_3a1_3ap_3a4-6.htm.
11 Boadway and Dougherty, *Decentralisation in a Globalised World,* 6, 8.

relations are between states and local governments to the exclusion of the federal government. Increasingly, however, local government is being seen as an integral part of federal governance.[12]

The classical model of federalism is premised on two orders of government: the federal government and the states (or provinces, *Länder*, or cantons). Local government was not usually recognized as an order of government but seen as a competence of the subnational units. Within the dual federalism model, in which there is a clear division of powers and functions, local government was typically placed within the sole jurisdiction of the states, excluding any direct federal interference. Local governments were mere creatures of states, existing at their will and having no independent relations with the federal government.[13]

Having said that, we can confirm that all federal countries have a local government tier, but its place and role in the governance of these countries varies considerably. In some countries, local government is considered an essential part of the federal nature of the state and recognized in the constitution as such, whereas in others it is simply a creature of the subnational states/provinces. When referring to local government, it is more correct to refer to local governments (plural), as these institutions come in all shapes and sizes, performing widely divergent functions. They range from metropolitan municipalities of megacities to counties, small town councils, and villages. Their focus is either multi-purpose, in the case of municipalities, or single purpose in the case of special districts and school districts. What unites these institutions of state is that there is no level of government below them. That is also their strength and the source of their democratic claim: they are the government closest to the people.[14]

---

12 Nico Steytler and John Kincaid, "Introduction," in *Local Government and Metropolitan Regions in Federal Countries*, ed. Nico Steytler and John Kincaid (Montreal: McGill-Queen's University Press, 2009), 3–6.
13 Steytler and Kincaid, eds., *Local Government and Metropolitan Regions in Federal Countries*, 393–436.
14 Ibid.

THE CHALLENGES FOR FEDERALISM AND THE FUTURE STRUCTURE OF FEDERAL STATES

A shared view of how to face the problems of the new century claims that the same local actors that created the new vital environment in many cities will be the ones who will transform the current urbanism into a more inclusive model. In this view little hope is invested in the possibility of central governments tackling these issues. From a federal point of view, the issue is usually seen more as a problem between the central and local governments, skipping the level of the subnational units. The underlying philosophy is that level of governments at which decision-making power resides should be closer to the people and that the nation-state will disappear in the near future, so the real axis of government will be the cities and metropolitan areas. Our concern, from a political perspective, is that cutting political sovereignty into pieces will imply a weakness political power that can be exercised by the citizens themselves.

Globalization plus the growing role of information technology economy imply a challenge for the traditional structures of federal or multilevel governments and a realignment of responsibilities for the different levels of governments. There are two forces that work in different ways. From one point of view, federal governments give decision-making powers to supranational organizations; from the other, local governments have greater stature in large urban areas since they are supposed to provide infrastructure and so-called social capital to serve as hubs in which innovation occurs. These elements will imply, according to some opinions, a reform in the near future in the federal and multilevel government systems by which government responsibilities will shift from state governments, both upward to central governments and downward to local governments (so-called "hourglass federalism").[15] According to this view, subnational units will be converted from primary providers of public services to supervisors of services that are delivered by local governments. If large cities play a crucial role in innovation and

---

15 " . . . namely the growing range of federal government initiatives that bypass the provinces and deal directly with citizens and cities, leaving the provinces as the squeezed middle of the division-of-powers hourglass, as it were." Thomas J. Courchene, "Hourglass Federalism—How the Feds Got the Provinces to Run Out Of Money in a Decade of Liberal Budgets," *Options Politiques* (April 2004), 12–17; see also Dorothée Allain-Dupré, *Assigning Responsibilities across Levels of Government: Trends, Challenges and Guiding Principles for Policy-makers*, OECD Fiscal Federalism Working Papers (Paris: OECD, 2018).

growth, their demands and needs for infrastructure and public services are very important. Establishing financial mechanisms that give them the ability and autonomy to implement infrastructure programs and local services to support the new knowledge economic activity is crucial. The difficulties lie in how to provide the local governments with the fiscal tools. The devolution of income or sales taxes to local governments or the implementation of block-grant programs or revenue-sharing mechanisms may be the alternatives. Another issue is that cities vary greatly in size, and within states one or two cities can dominate the populations. Therefore, the case for asymmetric treatment is strong (by giving only to the larger ones the access to revenue sources), but local equalization systems based on need and that distinguish among cities by population size are relatively easy to design.[16]

According to Robin Boadway and Sean Dougherty, fiscal federalism should follow the patterns explained below:

Federal government. It has a prime role to play in responding to challenges of inequality. It controls the personal tax-transfer system, which is the first tool to combat income and wealth inequality. The corporate tax system may be also used to encourage innovation investment and tax economic rents at source and design devices to attack base erosion and profit shifting through tax avoidance schemes. It also commands the main elements of the social and unemployment welfare system.[17] The federal tax policy can (partly) address the improvement of productivity, innovation, and entrepreneurship to pursue economic growth, by making business and personal taxes friendlier to investment and innovation. Federal governments are expected to deal with the inequality produced by globalization and with the enhancing of the skills needed to survive in a knowledge-based economy, which means assuming more responsibilities in the social welfare net, educating citizens, and encouraging innovation. All of this means federal leadership and cooperation with subnational governments, and a reinforcement of federal responsibilities that will come at the expense of state governments, which are traditionally in charge of social programs and education. In summary, the realignment of fiscal responsibilities will imply the recognition of the importance of the federal government role in addressing inequality, innovation, and human capital investment.

---

16 Boadway and Dougherty, *Decentralisation in a Globalised World*, 7.
17 Ibid.

State governments. These governments influence human capital investment through the universities and colleges that they usually operate. They usually control transportation facilities and communications technology. The realignment of responsibilities implies a shift from state governments, which will change their role of primary providers of public services to supervisors of services that are delivered by local governments. They will most probably become a conduit between the federal and the local governments, assuming a coordinating role with local governments in the provision of infrastructure, transportation, and education.[18]

Local governments. They are usually responsible for the larger amount of infrastructure spending. Cities, as pointed out before, are the hosting of innovation hubs and the high skilled persons employed by the high-tech sector. The urban areas are the place where technology networks work and local governments are the ones providing the public infrastructure that supports them. Thus, responsibilities of local governments grow in the same way as the urban areas grow. Local governments are the ones who have to provide the infrastructure and social capital to support and encourage this growth and also to serve as hubs in which innovation and human capital may develop. Thus, their role in the whole multilevel system will enhance both as providers of essential services and as the keepers in good conditions of the infrastructure. Therefore, the realignment of fiscal responsibilities will have to recognize the need for local governments to have the ability to provide infrastructure and innovative hubs (sometimes in collaboration with private institutions such as infrastructure banks or direct access to pension funds).[19] Financing local governments in order to improve local autonomy will imply giving enough revenue-raising ability to local governments so they are held responsible for budget shortfalls. This may include:[20]

> piggy-backing on state taxes,
>
> revenue sharing, and
>
> fiscal transfers.

---

18 Ibid., 8, 9.
19 Ibid., 8–10.
20 Ibid., 9–10.

In any case, as Boadway and Dougherty point out, history, diversity, political institutions, and culture will have an impact on the mechanisms to apply to the different countries.[21]

In the next sections there is a short overview of the situation in Australia and Canada, plus a short reference to the situation in the Basque Country. According to certain studies, Australia has a low relative local government importance, and Canada has an average or mixed relative local government importance. From the local autonomy perspective (taking into consideration the amount of revenue at the disposal of the local governments than can be used subject only to local government discretion), Canada and Australia are considered as having low local autonomy).[22]

AUSTRALIA

Local government is the third tier of government in Australia, although it is not recognized in the federal constitution. It is established under state laws, and all aspects of local administration are subject to detailed state control.[23] This means that each state government defines the powers of its local governments and decides for which geographical areas those local authorities are responsible. This third tier of government is consequently legislatively established at the state and territory (second-tier) level. In other words, the states are the primary "metropolitan managers."[24]

Australia has around 560 local government areas. They are extremely varied, with populations ranging from fewer than one hundred inhabitants to nearly one million, and areas from just 2 to almost 380,000 square kilometers. Overall, local government in Australia is relatively weak. Its activities are limited mostly to the provision of municipal services and local infrastructure, and its expenditures account for only 2.5 percent

---

21 Ibid., 10.
22 Harold Wolman and Diana Hincapie, "OECD Countries Local Government Fiscal Context," in *National Fiscal Policy and Local Government during the Economic Crisis*, vol. 2, *Country Profiles*, Urban Paper Series (Washington, D.C.: The German Marshall Fund of the United States, 2014), 1–4. The authors point out the one exception is the United States, where localism is very well founded both culturally and politically even though it is not institutionally embedded.
23 Graham Sansom, "Commonwealth of Australia," in *Local Government and Metropolitan Regions in Federal Countries*, ed. Steytler and Kincaid, 8–36.
24 Roberta Ryan and Ronald Woods, "Local Government Capacity in Australia," *Public Policy and Administration* 14, no. 3 (2015), 225–48.

of gross domestic product (GDP).[25] Local governments in Australia exhibit considerable diversity, not only in terms of their size and the demographic, geographic, and economic attributes of their LGAs (local government areas), but also due to the state-based legislative frameworks in which they operate, their financial capacities, the preferences and expectations of their local communities, and the management capacity and skills base of their elected representatives (councilors) and staff.[26]

During recent years, debates and practices relating to fiscal decentralization (namely, the devolution of authority for public finances and the delivery of government services from the national to subnational levels) has primarily been focused on the relations between the federal government and the state and territory governments. There has been no concerted policy direction in recent years to devolve greater levels of responsibility for policy making, management, and implementation of national goals to the municipalities.[27] However, even though local government is not an equal partner with the commonwealth and states/territories in terms of intergovernmental debates and agreements, it is difficult for higher tiers of governments to meet targets without involvement of local communities and local governments.

In recent years, there have been attempts to have local government formally recognized in the federal constitution, including plans for a national referendum on the issue in the period 2013–2014, but, as has often occurred in the past, the impetus for this waned.[28] Discussion of local government's role in democratic practice and as a vehicle for democratic legitimization gained renewed currency, especially in the context of neoliberal ideas about efficiency in service provision under network governance. Direct citizen participation in local democracy is often cited as a remedy for the weak democratic legitimacy and accountability deficits associated with network governance, outsourcing, and marketization. Local government is seen to be ideally placed as the locus of direct citizen involvement because of its local knowledge and existing community ties and because it is closest to the people.[29] However,

25 Sansom, "Commonwealth of Australia," in *Local Government and Metropolitan Regions in Federal Countries*, ed. Steytler and Kincaid.
26 Ryan and Woods, "Local Government Capacity in Australia," 231.
27 Ibid., 230 and 244.
28 Ibid., 238. See also Nicola Brackertz, "Political Actor or Policy Instrument? Governance Challenges in Australian Local Government," *Commonwealth Journal of Local Governance* 12 (May 2013), 3–19.
29 Brackertz, "Political Actor or Policy Instrument?" 10. The debate on the status of local government started in the 1970s with the election of the Gough Whitlam government and renewed debates around local government as a site of responsive

this position is still not entrenched in the constitutional framework, and the curious thing that some commentators observe is that there appears to be a persistent reluctance on the part of local government to take up its own cause and initiate change. This is evidenced, for example, by the fact that although local government peak bodies have initiated a number of inquiries, local government has been hesitant to put together an action package of reforms, leaving responses to the recommendations of inquires largely to state and federal governments.[30] But it is also true that there is growing acceptance in the local government sector that enhanced strategic capacity linked to factors such as increased size and resourcing levels, pooling of knowledge and expertise, and encouraging a focus on operating in a broader context appears essential to local government's long-term success as a valued partner in the federal system of government.[31]

Together with this, some voices[32] have arisen pointing out the "missing link" in Australia's reforms in recent years, since institutional restructuring in Australia has not been accompanied by intergovernmental decentralization (in contrast to what happened in the European Union[33]). This is especially relevant to global city strategies and also to Australia. Every state (except Tasmania and the Northern Territory) claims its capital cities are or should become global cities. The metropolitan impetus arising elsewhere from globalization is not felt in Australia. Australia has not created metropolitan governments. Consequently, there has been no debate by a metropolitan constituency about the desirability of a global city strategy. In effect, while Australia has embraced neoliberal institutional restructuring and state governments pursue global competitiveness as the foundation for urban policies, decentralization is not on the agenda. Metropolitan governance is discussed but metropolitan government is not.[34]

---

governance, democratization, and empowerment. In the 1980s, with the neoliberal wave of public sector reforms that swept all levels of the federal system that were characterized by managerialism, marketization, and the new public management, the cumulative effect was a strong emphasis on neoliberal economic and neoconservative political principles and a shift from "government" to "governance."

30 Brackertz, "Political Actor or Policy Instrument?" 15–16.
31 Ryan and Woods, "Local Government Capacity in Australia," 244.
32 Richard Tomlinson, "Metropolitan Regions are the Missing Link in Australia´s Reform Agenda," *The Conversation*, April 3, 2016, at https://theconversation.com/metropolitan-governance-is-the-missing-link-in-australias-reform-agenda-55872.
33 Anton Kreukels, Willem Salet, and Andy Thornley, eds., *Metropolitan Governance and Spatial Planning Comparative Case Studies of European City-Regions* (New York: Routledge, 2003).
34 On this concept see Saskia Sassen, *The Global City: New York, London, Tokyo*

CANADA

From the constitutional point of view, municipalities in Canada are creatures of the provinces, with no constitutional autonomy and no right to be consulted on provincial or federal government decisions that directly impact them. The provinces have the power to create, eliminate, and regulate municipalities. This is due to historical reasons. At the time of the British North America Act of 1867, Canada was predominantly rural, so urban affairs were not an issue of pressing substance.[35] Therefore, Canadian municipalities were defined under the 1867 Constitution (articles 92(2) and (8)) as administrative creatures of the provinces, that is, a Canadian municipality can only manage powers and revenue sources if its province has granted it, so in theory, the cities' subordination to provincial governments is absolute.[36] Today, although most Canadians live in cities, municipal governments' policymaking powers remain circumscribed to the provincial government.[37]

With all these limits, the story of municipal government in the Canadian federation is considered to be a success story. Stable local governments administer a wide range of services and provide public goods within a framework of democratic accountability. Canada has a long tradition of local control of municipal governments, which generally function adequately and efficiently. Despite some substantial changes, however, the essence of the system remains unaltered: the provincial governments control municipalities and what they do. Nevertheless, there are always issues that are under discussion and the last ones have produced a lively debate.[38]

Canada´s biggest cities are facing the sort of challenges that we have described before and that fall both within and outside of their institutional

---

(Princeton, NJ: Princeton University Press, 1991).

35 Conor Lewis, "Urban Governance and the Future of Canadian Federalism," *Federalism-E* 16 (2015), 2–9.

36 Michael Dewing, William R. Young, and Erin Tolley, *Municipalities, the Constitution, and the Canadian Federal System* ([Ottawa]: Parliamentary Information and Research Service, 2006), quoted in Herry-Saint-Onge et al., *Empowered Cities.*

37 Patrick Smith and Kennedy Stewart, "Local Whole-of-Government Policymaking in Vancouver," in *Canada: The State of the Federation 2004: Municipal-federal-provincial Relations in Canada* (Montreal: McGill-Queen´s University Press, 2006), 258, quoted in Lewis, "Urban Governance and the Future of Canadian Federalism," 3.

38 Robert Young, "Canada," in *Local Government and Metropolitan Regions in Federal Countries*, ed. Steytler and Kincaid, 107–35.

powers (such as aging infrastructure, integration of immigrants, housing, climate change, and so on). The control of all aspects of urban development is given to the provinces and these have simultaneously been amalgamating municipalities[39] while at the same time downloading programs dealing with the management of social diversity on the shoulders of urban cities; but without any increase in financial resources.[40] Thus, there has been a growing literature facing this issue that holds that if the urban cities were given the financial tools and the political powers to create their own social policy, they would be able to tackle them in a better way than the provinces since they "would approach the issues in a myriads of creative ways" and they would be a reimagining of the competitive era of federalism and creative asymmetry that would create new programs that could be replicated in other cities.[41]

From the viewpoint of cities as the centers of the new digital economy, the core idea is that what may happen to the Canadian cities is "more crucial than what goes in our mines, farms and fishing boats;"[42] and that the future relies on the critical role of so called Global City Regions.[43] The six largest metropolitan areas of Canada (Toronto, Vancouver, Montreal, Calgary, Edmonton, and Ottawa) are inhabited by 50 percent of the total Canadian population and generate half of the GDP, thus, the extended opinion that if Canada wants to be successful in the competitive framework of the global economy, it is crucial that its cities are successful too.[44]

---

39 According to some authors, "not so much for the better capacity of the municipality to act but for less expensive city government." See Caroline Andrew in "The Shame of (Ignoring) the Cities," *Journal of Canadian Studies* 7, no. 4 (2001), 105.

40 Andrew, "The Shame of (Ignoring) the Cities," 102. An example of amalgamation could be Hamilton, where five municipalities were joined together to form the city of Hamilton. One of the problems that derived from the amalgamation was that the former suburbs were given an equal place at the new city hall, but the issues that the suburban citizens wanted to address were totally different from the issues that worried the inner city citizens. See Lewis, "Urban Governance and the Future of Canadian Federalism," 3.

41 Thomas J. Courchene, "Global Futures for Canada's Global Cities," *IRPP Policy Matters* 8, no. 2 (2007), 27 and 1.

42 Andrew Sancton, "Beyond the Municipal: Governance for Canadian Cities," *Options Politiques* (February 2004), quoted in Conor, "Urban Governance and the Future of Canadian Federalism," 4.

43 Courchene, "Global Futures for Canada's Global Cities," 27 and 1, quoted by Lewis, "Urban Governance and the Future of Canadian Federalism," 2.

44 Adam Kahane and Anna Golden, "On Healthy Cities: We Will Fail If We Don't Invest in the Changes That Are Needed," *The Globe and Mail*, December 19, 2014, quoted in Herry-Saint-Onge et al., *Empowered Cities*, 4.

However, it is a common complaint that Canada turned a blind eye to the globalized, knowledge-based economy and the fundamental role that the aforementioned Global City Regions play as the motors of the digital economy. The underfunding of regional economic hubs limits the possibilities of creativity urban municipalities.[45] The majority of municipalities obtain their revenue from property taxes, which is not enough to satisfy the needs of the global city regions. Therefore, the idea of increasing the bases of taxation for municipalities is gaining ground. But most of the efforts to seek alternative strategies to the recognition of their political and economic importance, expanding their participation in the policymaking affecting their population and to increase their capacity of collecting taxes have fallen short.[46]

Some steps were taken in the past, though: milestones such as the New Deal, introduced in 2004, which gave municipalities a new role since this deal was looking for a redefinition of relationships among the three orders of government, providing more effective program support for infrastructure and social priorities. During its implementation (via the Ministry of Infrastructure), a percentage of the federal gas tax was redirected to the cities, but the New Deal was finally dissolved with the incoming government. On the other hand, some provinces have given their biggest cities more powers and a particular status through charters such as Vancouver in 1953, Toronto in 2006, and Montreal in 2008. Calgary and Edmonton are negotiating with Alberta.[47]

However, no matter how important these achievements may be, in order for cities to become economic and cultural hubs, they would probably need to be given the constitutional authority to communicate with the federal and provincial government. This would imply a "dual devolution of powers" (competences and resources would go from the federal government to the provinces and from the provinces to the local powers), which could be done through intergovernmental agreements enshrined into law. Maintaining the current constitutional division of powers seems to be for certain authors like keeping a relic from the colonial past. The rigid constitutional interpretation regarding the municipal level

---

45   Courchene, "Global Futures for Canada's Global Cities," 27 and 1, quoted by Lewis, "Urban Governance and the Future of Canadian Federalism," 2.

46   See Jean-Pierre Collin and Jacques Léveillée, *Municipal Organization in Canada: Tradition and Transformation, Varying From Province to Province* (Barcelona and Montréal: Diputació de Barcelona and Villes Régions Monde, 2003), quoted in Herry-Saint-Onge et al., *Empowered Cities: A New Path to Collaborative Federalism*, 4.

47   Herry-Saint-Onge et al., *Empowered Cities*, 4–5.

strengthens the continued suppression of urban governance and keeps the current division of powers within the federation without adapting to the reality of urbanization.[48]

What it is not clear for scholars is whether there should be a constitutional reform in order to recognize the importance of the municipalities' role within the federation. It has been pointed out that constitutional amendments have become a political "non-starter." Some scholars recommend neither changing the Constitution nor the current legal status of the cities, but a "more collaborative federalism," that is, one in which the different orders of government work together as equals in a partnership to find solutions to the country´s challenges, which are increasingly manifesting themselves in Canada´s biggest cities.[49] This position claims that the customary practices of federalism have been able to evolve according to the developments in Canada. Thus, now an evolution is required to modernize the relationships between Canada´s cities and the federal and provincial governments. In other words, what is needed is a change in governance culture that can go beyond the jurisdictional limitations to a more collaborative federalism. The call for an enhancement of municipal leadership and intergovernmental relations will improve Canadian federalism and will give Canadian big cities the political weight they need to tackle the challenges of the twenty-first century.[50]

SHORT DISCUSSION OF THE BASQUE COUNTRY

The legal-institutional structure of the Autonomous Community of the Basque Country (Euskadi) is based on the structuring of three institutional levels: the common institutions (Basque government and parliament), the Historical Territories (Bizkaia, Gipuzkoa, and Araba), and the municipalities and other local entities. The legal framework is constituted by the Spanish Constitution, the Statute of Autonomy, the Economic Agreement, and the Law of Historical Territories.

The recent approval of Law 2/2016, of April 7, of Local Institutions of Euskadi, has come to provide the Basque municipalities for a legal framework that gives them stability and allows them to exercise their self-

---

48 Lewis, "Urban Governance and the Future of Canadian Federalism," 2.
49 Herry-Saint-Onge et al., *Empowered Cities*, 8.
50 Ibid.

government and fulfill its main purpose, that is, to meet the demands of citizens in their condition of the closest administrations to the citizens.[51] The law provides clarity to the economic-financial framework in which the activity of the local entities must be developed, foreseeing the essential presence of Basque municipalities in the bodies and decision-making processes that affect them directly. Therefore, it results in a situation in which these administrations are subject to a degree of tutelage not always respectful of the relevant functions that correspond to them and not always compatible with authentic respect for local autonomy that municipalities should have guaranteed in accordance with constitutional principles.[52]

However, the law establishes the exclusive attribution to the Historical Territories the competence to determine the municipal participation in the resources derived from the Economic Agreement. In other words, the determination of which participation corresponds in each Historical Territory to each of its local entities is the competence of the Historical Territories. Consequently, they will exercise it freely, subject to what it is established in the regional norms and in the decisions made by the Basque Council of Public Finances referred to the exercise of their attributions in budgetary stability matters and to guarantee the financial stability of the municipalities. Ultimately, after the approval of the abovementioned law, it can be affirmed that the Historical Territories, through their competencies over the local treasuries, clearly affect both the tax aspects (local taxes, participation in agreed taxes) and budgetary aspects (authorizations of indebtedness, reports, regulation of criteria and approval of economic-financial plans) of the municipalities.[53]

The new law does not foresee a specific status for the type of metropolis we mentioned before. This may be due to the fact that there are no really big cities in the Basque Country together with the idea of balancing the resources between the different territories and municipalities. The idea of promoting specific urban locations for innovation is not only targeted for the cities (for example, Bilbao) but also for the Historical Territories (for example, Bizkaia). On the other hand, there is a mixture of different goals that, although they may work as synergies on the

---

51 We basically follow in this section José G. Rubí Casinello, "La financiación municipal en el País Vasco y la Ley de Instituciones Locales de Euskadi," *Zergak: Gaceta tributaria del País Vasco* 51, 111–26.

52 Ibid., 111.

53 Ibid., 120–23.

infrastructures they need, may also weaken the sleeked targets (for example, innovation vs. tourism).

FINAL REMARKS

There seems to be a common view (both from academia and the economic world), that federal (an unitary) states need to strengthen the powers of cities and metropolitan areas, facilitating the decentralization of responsibilities to urban governments.

However, there are important issues that we must question before joining the common view of the possibilities that the cities may bring to the welfare of their citizens and the optimism of this view of the future. It is remarkable to observe that it is becoming a common place to consider the nation-state almost as a political zombie of the twenty-first century, and the accent is not put on supra-international federal governance but on megacities, that is, kinds of new city-states. The opinion is very much founded on a democratic principle: the closer the representatives to the people are, the more accountable the former will be. Nevertheless, provided the constant trend to globalization of MNEs (multinational entities) and the power it brings, it seems as though the power of citizens and ordinary people will not be increased by transferring certain powers to their municipalities. If states cannot survive because they are too weak and cannot accommodate to the new requirements of the twenty-first century, it is still not clear for us whether megacities can take the lead and sail alone through the troubled waters of globalization.

In our opinion, the optimistic view that the new forms of metropolitan governance and decentralization of roles and responsibilities is a response to the difficulties and new challenges arising from globalization does not fit with reality. The idea that infrastructure investment and services and partnerships with the private sector and civil society are best led by a representative and accountable urban government sounds reasonable but has its limits. The bargaining power of metropolises, no matter how big they are, cannot be compared to the negotiation power of a whole country. If the cities are going to be the service providers under the supervision of the subnational units and the direct accountability of its citizens, we would better provide them with the necessary negotiation framework to acquire the best partners that will fill their needs at a reasonable cost.

Further, there seems to be a contradiction between the natural acceptance of global economic players (MNEs) and local political characters (no matter how "global" the cities are). Global multinational actors drive the economy and build the infrastructure (both physical and intangible infrastructures). Metropolises are not in an equal position to negotiate. The solution may be in the cities´ nets, which are improving and expanding dramatically. Still, there seems to be a contradiction between the defense of local players (no matter how interconnected they may be) facing multinational interlocutors and the subtle rejection of supra-federal powers. In this regard, the extent to which the federal government should have direct fiscal relations with larger cities remains an open question,[54] especially since their policies can have national implications.

The will for more financial resources and responsibilities and also more political weight in the federal structure is a reasonable demand. However, the changes needed have to be carefully designed and implemented and giving to the cities the prominence they deserve without weakening the synergies of subnational units and the advantages of a powerful federal state.

BIBLIOGRAPHY

Allain-Dupré, Dorothée. *Assigning Responsibilities across Levels of Government: Trends, Challenges and Guiding Principles for Policy-makers.* OECD Fiscal Federalism Working Papers. Paris: OECD, 2018.

Allers, Maarten A. "Yardstick Competition, Fiscal Disparities, and Equalization." *Economics Letters* 117, no. 1 (2012): 4–6. At https://econpapers.repec.org/article/eeeecolet/v_3a117_3ay_3 a2012_3ai_3a1_3ap_3a4-6.htm.

---

54 As is pointed out by Boadway and Dougherty, *Decentralisation in a Globalised World*, 10. They also point out other important issues that have to be solved under this perspective, namely: The role of decentralization in local governments and particularly local infrastructure on growth; inequality and other dimensions of inclusive growth; and the performance record of institutions like private-public partnerships, infrastructure banks, and fiscal councils.

Andrew, Caroline. "The Shame of (Ignoring) the Cities." *Journal of Canadian Studies* 7, no. 4 (2001): 100–110.

Ascher, Francois. *Los nuevos principios del urbanismo*. Madrid: Alianza, 2004.

Battelle, John. "Can Business and New Federalism Save our Cities?" *Newco Shift*, September 14, 2017. At https://shift.newco.co/can-business-and-new-federalism-save-our-cities-e5926997f578.

Boadway, Robin, and Sean Dougherty. *Decentralisation in a Globalised World: Consequences and Opportunities*. OECD Working Papers on Fiscal Federalism, No. 21. Paris: OECD, 2018.

Brackertz, Nicola. "Political Actor or Policy Instrument? Governance Challenges in Australian Local Government." *Commonwealth Journal of Local Governance* 12 (May 2013): 3–19.

Collin, Jean-Pierre, and Jacques Léveillée. *Municipal Organization in Canada: Tradition and Transformation, Varying From Province to Province*. Barcelona and Montréal: Diputació de Barcelona and Villes Régions Monde, 2003.

Courchene, Thomas J. "Global Futures for Canada´s Global Cities." *IRPP Policy Matters* 8, no. 2 (2007): 1–36.

———. "Hourglass Federalism: How the Feds got the Provinces to Run out of Money in a Decade of Liberal Budgets." *Options Politiques* (April 2004): 12–17.

Dewing, Michael, William R. Young, and Erin Tolley. *Municipalities, the Constitution, and the Canadian Federal System*. [Ottawa]: Parliamentary Information and Research Service, 2006.

Dougherty, Sean M., and Oguzhan Akgun, "Globalisation, Decentralization and Inclusive Growth." In *Fiscal Decentralisation and Inclusive Growth*, edited by Sean M. Dougherty and Junghun Kim. Paris: OECD/KPF, 2018.

Florida, Richard. *The Rise of the Creative Class: And How It's Transforming Work, Leisure, Community and Everyday Life*. New York: Basic Books, 2002.

Herry-Saint-Onge, Véronique, Morvan Le Borgne, Jesse Kancir, Emilie Nicolas, André Juneau, and James Stuewe. *Empowered Cities: A New Path to Collaborative Federalism*. N.p.: Action Canada, 2015.

Kreukels, Anton, Willem Salet, and Andy Thornley Andy, eds. *Metropolitan Governance and Spatial Planning Comparative Case Studies of European City-Regions*. New York: Routledge, 2003.

Kahane, Adam, and Anna Golden. "On Healthy Cities: We Will Fail If We Don´t Invest in the Changes That Are Needed." *The Globe and Mail*, December 19, 2014.

Lewis, Conor. "Urban Governance and the Future of Canadian Federalism." *Federalism-E* 16 (2015): 2–9.

Lucio Gil, Antonio. "Ciudades: El escenario en el que nos jugamos el future," Cambio climático: El Planeta Atormentado 18, supplement, *eldiario.es* (online newspaper), April 2, 2018.

Organisation for Economic Co-operation and Development (OECD). *All on Board: Making Inclusive Growth Happen*. Paris: OECD Publishing, 2015.

Rubí Casinello, José G. "La financiación municipal en el País Vasco y la Ley de Instituciones Locales de Euskadi." *Zergak: Gaceta tributaria del País Vasco* 51 (2017): 111–26.

Ryan, Roberta, and Ronald Woods. "Local Government Capacity in Australia." *Public Policy and Administration* 14, no. 3 (2015): 225–48.

Sancton, Andrew. "Beyond the Municipal: Governance for Canadian Cities." *Options Politiques* (February 2004): 26–31.

Sansom, Graham. "Commonwealth of Australia." In *Local Government and Metropolitan Regions in Federal Countries*, edited by Nico Steytler and John Kincaid. Montreal: McGill-Queen's University Press, 2009.

Sassen, Saskia. *The Global City: New York, London, Tokyo*. Princeton, NJ: Princeton University Press, 1991.

Smith, Patrick, and Kennedy Stewart. "Local Whole-of-Government Policymaking in Vancouver." In *Canada: The State of the Federation 2004: Municipal-federal-provincial Relations in Canada*. Montreal: McGill-Queen´s University Press, 2006.

Steytler, Nico, and John Kincaid, eds. "Introduction." In *Local Government and Metropolitan Regions in Federal Countries*, edited by Nico Steytler and John Kincaid, Montreal: McGill-Queen's University Press, 2009.

Tomlinson, Richard. "Metropolitan Regions Are the Missing Link in Australia's Reform Agenda." *The Conversation*, April 3, 2016. At https://theconversation.com/metropolitan-governance-is-the-missing-link-in-australias-reform-agenda-55872.

Wolman, Harold, and Diana Hincapie. "OECD Countries Local Government Fiscal Context." In *National Fiscal Policy and Local Government during the Economic Crisis*. Volume 2. *Country Profiles*. Urban Paper Series. Washington, D.C.: The German Marshall Fund of the United States, 2014.

World Economic Forum. *The Competiveness of Cities*. Geneva: World Economic Forum, 2014.

Young, Robert. "Canada." In *Local Government and Metropolitan Regions in Federal Countries*, edited by Steytler and Kincaid. Montreal: McGill-Queen's University Press, 2009.